WW2 – THE PACIFIC WAR

AMAZING FACTS, KEY PLAYERS, HEROIC ACTS, MAJOR BATTLES, AND HOW THE WAR CHANGED THE WORLD

James Burrows

© **Copyright 2025 - All rights reserved.**

The content contained within this book may not be reproduced, duplicated or transmitted without direct written permission from the author or the publisher.

Under no circumstances will any blame or legal responsibility be held against the publisher, or author, for any damages, reparation, or monetary loss due to the information contained within this book, either directly or indirectly.

Legal Notice:

This book is copyright protected. It is only for personal use. You cannot amend, distribute, sell, use, quote or paraphrase any part, or the content within this book, without the consent of the author or publisher.

Disclaimer Notice:

Please note the information contained within this document is for educational and entertainment purposes only. All effort has been executed to present accurate, up to date, reliable, complete information. No warranties of any kind are declared or implied. Readers acknowledge that the author is not engaged in the rendering of legal, financial, medical or professional advice. The content within this book has been derived from various sources. Please consult a licensed professional before attempting any techniques outlined in this book.

By reading this document, the reader agrees that under no circumstances is the author responsible for any losses, direct or indirect, that are incurred as a result of the use of the information contained within this document, including, but not limited to, errors, omissions, or inaccuracies.

Other Books by James Burrows

What You Need To Know:

World War I for Teens
World War I for Kids
World War II for Teens
World War II for Kids
World War II for Teens – 21 Special Operations
World War II for Teens – The Secret War
World War II for Teens – The Holocaust
World War II – The Pacific War
The Vietnam War for Teens

The Ultimate Guide:

Egyptian Mythology for Kids
Greek Mythology for Kids
Norse Mythology for Kids

Concise Guides:

A History of Israel and Palestine
Alexander the Great - One Man. One Empire. One Legacy.

Other Books:

The Art of War – Sun Tzu
Meditations – Marcus Aurelius

CONTENTS

INTRODUCTION

CHAPTER 1: WELCOME TO THE PACIFIC WAR

Major Theatres of the Pacific War

Significance of the Pacific Theatre

The Human Cost

Post-War Changes

CHAPTER 2: THE ROAD TO WAR

The Meiji Restoration and Japan's Modernization

The Rise of Japanese Nationalism

The Need for Resources and Expansion – "The Greater East Asia Co-Prosperity Sphere"

Growing tensions with other powers

The Road to Pearl Harbor

CHAPTER 3: TIMELINE OF MAJOR EVENTS AND BATTLES

CHAPTER 4: WAR PLANS

Japan's Strategy in World War II

Pre-War Planning

Early War Strategy

Mid-War Adjustments

Late-War Strategy

America's War Plans: From Defense to Counterattack

The Battle for the Pacific Begins

CHAPTER 5: THE BRUTAL REALITY OF THE PACIFIC WAR

The Terrain: An Unforgiving Environment

Extreme Weather: A Relentless Adversary

Psychological Strain

The Brutality of Combat

Disease and Starvation: The Silent Killers

CHAPTER 6: MAP OF THE PACIFIC CAMPAIGN

CHAPTER 7: KEY LEADERS AND GENERALS

Allied Leaders

General Douglas MacArthur: The "American Caesar"

Admiral Chester W. Nimitz: The Master Strategist

Admiral William "Bull" Halsey Jr.: The Aggressive Commander

General Joseph "Vinegar Joe" Stilwell: The China-Burma-India Commander

General Holland M. "Howlin' Mad" Smith: The Father of Modern Amphibious Warfare

Admiral Raymond A. Spruance: The Quiet Strategist

Admiral Lord Louis Mountbatten: The Southeast Asia Commander

General Sir William Slim: The "Forgotten Army" Commander

Chiang Kai-shek: The Leader of Nationalist China

Axis Leaders

Admiral Isoroku Yamamoto: The Architect of Pearl Harbor

General Hideki Tojo: The Prime Minister

General Tadamichi Kuribayashi: The Defender of Iwo Jima

Admiral Chuichi Nagumo: The Carrier Fleet Commander

General Masaharu Homma: The Conqueror of the Philippines

General Tomoyuki Yamashita: The "Tiger of Malaya"

Admiral Takeo Kurita: The Commander at Leyte Gulf

CHAPTER 8: THE ATTACK ON PEARL HARBOR – THE WAR BEGINS

Japan's Gamble: The Plan to Strike First

The Attack: A Perfectly Executed Ambush

The Aftermath: America Awakens

How the U.S. Underestimated The Threat From Japan

The Toll on The Pacific Fleet: A Navy in Ruins

The Airfields: The Sky Lost Before It Could Fight

The Shockwaves of Pearl Harbor: A Nation Transformed

CHAPTER 9: EARLY JAPANESE VICTORIES AND BRITISH DEFEATS

The Fall of Hong Kong: A Symbolic Loss (December 8–25, 1941)

The Invasion of the Philippines (December 8, 1941 – May 1942)

The Malayan Campaign: A Blitzkrieg in the Jungle (December 8, 1941 – February 15, 1942)

The Battle for Singapore (February 1942): The Final Stand

Wake Island (December 8 – 23, 1941)

Thailand and Indochina (December 1941)

Guam (December 8 – 10, 1941)

Rabaul (January 23, 1942)

The Burma Campaign: A Retreat into the Jungle (January–May 1942)

The Japanese Invasion of the Dutch East Indies (January – March 1942)

A Time of Triumph for Japan

CHAPTER 10: THE FIRST TURNING POINT – THE BATTLE OF THE CORAL SEA

The U.S. Navy: A Fleet Rebuilding

The Imperial Japanese Navy: A Force on the Offensive

The Rise of Carrier Warfare

The Human Element: Courage and Sacrifice

Initial Actions: Setting the Stage

Carrier Engagement: A Clash of Air Power

The Aftermath: A Strategic Turning Point

CHAPTER 11: THE BATTLE OF MIDWAY

The Intelligence Breakthrough: How the U.S. Knew Japan's Plans

The Battle Begins: June 3–4, 1942

The Turning Point: America's Carrier Strikes (June 4, 1942, Morning)

The Final Blow: The Sinking of Hiryū (June 4–5, 1942)

The Human Cost: Death and Survival

Why Midway Changed the War

CHAPTER 12: THE ISLAND HOPPING CAMPAIGN

The Battle of Guadalcanal (August 7, 1942 – February 9, 1943)

Battle of Tarawa (November 20 – 23, 1943): The First Test of Island Hopping

Battle of Kwajalein (January 31 – February 3, 1944): The First Breakthrough

Battle of Saipan, Tinian, and Guam (June 15 – July 9, 1944): A Step Toward Japan Itself

Battle of Peleliu (September 15 – November 27, 1944)

The Battle for the Philippines: MacArthur's Return (October 1944 – August 1945)

The Battle of Leyte Gulf (October 23 – 26, 1944)

CHAPTER 13: THE BRITISH CAMPAIGN IN BURMA

Geography: A Land of Jungle and Mountains

Resources: A Prize Worth Fighting For

Allied Strategy: Protecting India and Supporting China

Japanese Success

The Road to Liberation (January 1944 – November 1994)

Role of General William Slim

Harsh Conditions

Impact of the Japanese Retreat

CHAPTER 14: THE BATTLE OF IWO JIMA

Allied Objectives: A Stepping Stone and a Lifeline

The Island's Geography: A Natural Fortress

The Human Cost: A Battle of Attrition

The Japanese Defenders: Dug-in and Determined

The U.S. Marines: Island Hopping Veterans

Key Phases of the Battle

CHAPTER 15: THE BATTLE OF OKINAWA

The Japanese Defenses: A Fortress of Death

The Fight for Shuri Castle: The Bloodiest Land Battle of the Pacific

Prolonged Fighting: A Grueling Struggle

Final Stages: The Fall of Okinawa

The Final Days: Japan's Last Stand

Shaping History - The Battle That Shaped the Atomic Bomb Decision

CHAPTER 16: THE RACE TO JAPAN AND THE ATOMIC BOMBS - THE ENDGAME (1945)

The "Ketsu-Go" Strategy: A Nation Mobilized for War

The Dilemma: Invasion or Alternative?

The Tokyo Firebombing (March 9-10, 1945): The Deadliest Air Raid

The Manhattan Project: Creating the Bomb

The Debate: Bomb or Invasion?

The Final Decision: Drop the Bomb

The Atomic Bombings: The Day the World Changed

Japan's Surrender: The End of World War II

The Day the World Changed Forever

The World Reacts

CHAPTER 17: WHY JAPAN'S STRATEGY FAILED

Fighting on Too Many Fronts

Economic and Industrial Limitations

Strategic Missteps

Technological and Tactical Disadvantages

Loss of Naval and Air Superiority

Internal Political and Social Issues

Allied Technological Superiority

CHAPTER 18: HEROES OF THE PACIFIC WAR

U.S. Marine Corporal Charles W. Lindberg (Iwo Jima)

Private Desmond T. Doss - The Hero of Hacksaw Ridge, Okinawa

U.S. Navy Chief Petty Officer Doris Miller - Hero of Pearl Harbor

British Indian Army Sepoy Kamal Ram - Victoria Cross Hero of Burma

Private First Class Eugene B. Sledge - A Marine's Story of Survival and Sacrifice

U.S. Army Technician Fifth Grade John R. Towle - Hero of the Leyte Campaign

The Chindits - Guerrilla Warfare in Burma

U.S. Army Rangers - The Cabanatuan Raid: A Daring POW Rescue

Lieutenant Commander Ernest E. Evans - Defiance at Leyte Gulf

Sergeant Major Jacob Vouza - The Indomitable Scout of Guadalcanal

Lieutenant John F. Kennedy and PT-109: A Test of Leadership

Filipino Guerrillas: The Resistance Against Japanese Occupation

Nurses and Medics - Unsung Heroes of the Pacific War

CHAPTER 19: WAR CRIMES AND THE COST OF WAR

The Bataan Death March (April 1942): A Journey of Suffering

The Burma Railway: The "Death Railway" of the Pacific

The Infamous Bridge on the River Kwai

Wake Island

Hell Ships

China and the Three Alls Policy

POW Stories of Survival

War Trials: Holding Japan's leaders accountable

The Nuremberg Trials: Justice for the Holocaust and War Crimes

The Tokyo Trials: Holding Japan's Leaders Accountable

The Legacy of the Trials: A New Standard for War Crimes

The Human Cost: The Staggering Death Toll of the Pacific War

The Death Toll by Nation and Region

The Civilian Experience: Starvation, Bombings, and Survival

The Psychological Toll: The Never-Ending War

CHAPTER 20: THE POST-WAR PACIFIC

The Occupation of Japan: MacArthur's reforms and rebuilding Japan (1945 – 1952)

General Douglas MacArthur: The Man Who Rebuilt Japan

Japan's Economic Miracle: The Rise of a Superpower

The Legacy of the Occupation

The Fall of European Empires in Asia: Decolonization and Independence

Independence Movements Across Asia

The Global Impact of Decolonization in Asia

LESSONS FROM THE PACIFIC WAR

ABOUT THE AUTHOR

INTRODUCTION

In the early hours of December 7, 1941, a day that would forever be etched in history, the tranquillity of a Pacific paradise was shattered. The U.S. naval base at Pearl Harbor, nestled amidst the serene beauty of Hawaii, became the target of a surprise aerial assault, launched by the Imperial Japanese Navy. The roar of aircraft engines pierced the morning calm, followed by the deafening explosions of bombs and torpedoes. Within minutes, the once mighty U.S. Pacific Fleet lay in ruins, its battleships ablaze, its aircraft reduced to twisted wreckage. The attack on Pearl Harbor marked the beginning of a new and devastating chapter in human history—the Pacific War.

The Pacific War, a theater of World War II, was a conflict unlike any other. It was a clash of civilizations, a struggle for dominance in a region where empires clashed and ideologies collided. It was a war that spanned vast distances, from the icy Aleutian Islands to the sweltering jungles of Southeast Asia, from the coral atolls of the Pacific to the foothills of the Himalayas. It was a war that tested the limits of human endurance, where soldiers fought not only against a determined enemy but also against the unforgiving forces of nature.

The Pacific War was a crucible that forged heroes and martyrs, where ordinary individuals rose to extraordinary heights of courage and sacrifice. It was a conflict that reshaped the geopolitical landscape of the world, ending Japan's imperial ambitions and paving the way for its transformation into a peaceful, democratic nation. It was a war that left an indelible mark on the human psyche, a reminder of the destructive potential of humanity and the enduring quest for peace.

What This Book Covers

This book will take you on a journey through the Pacific War, from its origins to its aftermath. We will explore:

- The key battles that shaped the war, from the devastating attack on Pearl Harbor to the brutal island-hopping campaigns and the final push toward Japan.

- The strategies used by both sides, including Japan's rapid expansion and the U.S. Navy's counteroffensive.

- The experiences of the soldiers, sailors, and pilots who fought in the jungles, on the beaches, and in the skies.

- The human cost of war, including the suffering of civilians, prisoners of war, and those caught in the crossfire.

- The impact of the atomic bombings and how they changed the course of history.

- The legacy of the Pacific War, shaping modern geopolitics, military strategy, and global relationships.

And look out for 'Did You Know' incredible war facts throughout the book, some amazing, and some just plain weird!

▫ *DID YOU KNOW*

- Estimates of the number of people who died in the Pacific War during World War II range from 25 million to over 35 million. This includes both military and civilian deaths.

- A Japanese soldier, Hiroo Onoda, refused to believe Japan had surrendered in 1945. He continued hiding in the jungles of the Philippines until 1974, when his former commanding officer personally ordered him to stand down.

- Many people don't realize that Australia was bombed 97 times by Japan, with the worst attack being the Bombing of Darwin in 1942. It was the largest foreign attack on Australian soil in history.

Our journey begins with an examination of the events that led to the outbreak of war in the Pacific. We will explore Japan's rise as a modern military power, its imperial ambitions in Asia, and the growing tensions with the United States and other Western powers. We will analyze the key decision points that ultimately led to the fateful attack on Pearl Harbor, plunging the United States into a war that would transform the nation and the world.

From the ashes of Pearl Harbor, we will trace the course of the war across the vast Pacific Theater. We will witness the early Japanese victories that stunned the world, the turning points that shifted the momentum in favor of the Allies, and the final, bloody battles that brought the war to a close. We will explore the innovative strategies and tactics employed by both sides, from the daring carrier battles of the Coral Sea and Midway to the grueling island-hopping campaigns across the Pacific.

The Pacific War was a conflict of immense human suffering. We will not shy away from exploring the brutal realities of combat, the physical and psychological toll it took on those who fought, and the devastating impact it had on civilians caught in the crossfire. We will examine the horrors of prisoner-of-war camps, the atrocities committed against civilians, and the desperate measures taken by both sides as the war reached its climax.

Yet, amidst the darkness of war, we will also find stories of hope, resilience, and compassion. We will witness the unwavering camaraderie among soldiers, the selfless acts of medics and nurses who risked their lives to save others, and the indomitable spirit of civilians who endured unimaginable hardships.

As we approach the end of our journey, we will reflect on the lasting legacy of the Pacific War. We will explore its impact on the geopolitical landscape of the world, the rise of the United States as a superpower, and the decline of European colonial empires. We will examine the war's profound influence on Japanese society, its transformation into a pacifist nation, and its complex relationship with the United States in the postwar era.

A Journey into History

The Pacific War was a defining moment in the 20th century. It was a war of ambition and destruction, but also of heroism and resilience. As you turn the pages of this book, you will step into the world of 1941-1945, experiencing the triumphs and tragedies of those who lived through it.

This is their story. And now, it is yours to discover.

CHAPTER 1: WELCOME TO THE PACIFIC WAR

World War II (1939–1945) was one of the most devastating and transformative events in human history. It involved over 30 countries and more than 100 million military personnel, making it the largest and deadliest conflict the world had ever seen. Beyond its staggering death toll - estimated at 70 - 85 million people, or about 3% of the world's population - World War II reshaped nations, ideologies, economies, and geopolitics.

The Pacific War (1941–1945) was one of the two main theaters of WWII - the other being Europe. While countries in Europe (like Germany, Italy, and Britain) were fighting it out, another huge battle was happening in the Pacific, mainly between Japan and the Allied Powers (including the United States, China, Britain, Australia, and others). It was a critical part of World War II and encompassed naval, air, and land battles across vast areas of the Pacific Ocean and Asia.

The Pacific War was rooted in Japan's imperial ambitions and aggressive expansionism during the early 20th century, where it sought to establish dominance in Asia and the Pacific by creating a "Greater East Asia Co-Prosperity Sphere." This vision involved conquering and exploiting resource-rich regions like China, Southeast Asia, and the Pacific islands.

This aggressive expansionism created tensions with western powers, with Japan's invasion of Manchuria (1931) and China (1937) straining relations with the U.S., Britain, and other Western powers. Economic sanctions were imposed, including the U.S. oil embargo in 1941, and this helped to push Japan toward more aggressive actions to secure resources.

Major Theaters of the Pacific War

The Pacific War was fought over a vast area, that can be divided into 5 'Theaters' (Theater is a term used for a large geographical area where military operations take place during a conflict), each with their own challenges. By organizing conflicts into theaters, military leaders could coordinate operations more effectively, ensuring that resources, strategy, and command structures were properly allocated to different regions.

1. Central Pacific

The Central Pacific Theater encompassed a vast area of the Pacific Ocean, stretching from the Hawaiian Islands in the east to the Mariana Islands and the Philippines in the west. This area was strategically vital for both the Allies and Japan, as it contained key islands that served as stepping stones for advances toward Japan and its vital territories in Southeast Asia.

The Central Pacific was the primary route for the Allies' island-hopping campaign, a strategy aimed at capturing key islands and using them as bases to advance closer to Japan. This campaign involved a series of amphibious assaults, naval battles, and air campaigns, culminating in the invasion of the Japanese home islands.

For Japan, it was a crucial defensive perimeter, protecting its access to vital resources in Southeast Asia and its communication lines with its forces in the South Pacific. Japan heavily fortified key islands, hoping to slow the Allied advance and inflict heavy casualties, potentially forcing a negotiated peace.

This area saw some of the most well-known battles of the Pacific War, including Midway, the Mariana Islands campaign, Iwo Jima, and Okinawa.

2. Southwest Pacific

Encompassing the islands of New Guinea, the Philippines, and the Solomon Islands, this was a battleground for a grueling and strategically vital struggle between the Allies and Japan. Characterized by dense jungles, rugged terrain, and treacherous seas, the Southwest Pacific Theater tested the limits of human endurance and played a crucial role in the Allied victory over Japan.

The Southwest Pacific Theater was strategically vital for both the Allies and Japan. For the Allies, it was a key link in their supply lines to Australia and a stepping stone for their advance toward the Philippines and Japan. For Japan, it was a defensive perimeter, protecting its access to vital resources in Southeast Asia and its communication lines with its forces in the South Pacific.

This was the scene of some of the most challenging and hard-fought campaigns of the Pacific War, including New Guinea and jungle warfare at its harshest, the Philippines, and the Solomon Islands.

3. ◻Southeast Asia

A fierce and often forgotten struggle raged in Southeast Asia. Encompassing the dense jungles of Burma (now Myanmar), the strategically vital Malay Peninsula, and the resource-rich Dutch East Indies (now Indonesia), this was a battleground for a complex and brutal conflict that involved not only the major powers but also local resistance movements and colonial forces.

For Japan, the region was crucial for its resource needs, providing access to vital raw materials such as oil, rubber, tin, and rice. Controlling Southeast Asia was also essential for Japan's goal of establishing a "Greater East Asia Co-Prosperity Sphere," a bloc of Asian nations under Japanese domination.

For the Allies, Southeast Asia represented a critical front in their efforts to contain Japanese expansion and support their allies, particularly China. The Burma Road, a vital supply route linking India to China, traversed Burma, making the region crucial for maintaining the flow of aid to the Chinese resistance against Japan.

Fighting occurred in Burma, Malaya, and the Dutch East Indies, and spanned jungle warfare, amphibious assaults, and aerial bombardments.

4. ◻China Theater

While the Pacific War is often associated with island battles and naval engagements, a vast and brutal conflict raged on the Asian mainland, in the China Theater. This was a protracted and devastating war between Japan and China, with the latter receiving crucial support from Allied nations, particularly the United States.

Japan had a long-held ambition of conquering China, driven by a desire for resources, territory, and regional dominance. China's vast population and resources represented a valuable prize.

For the Allies, China was a crucial ally in the fight against Japan. China's resistance tied down a significant portion of Japan's military forces, preventing them from being deployed elsewhere in the Pacific. Supporting China was also seen as a moral imperative, as the Chinese people suffered immensely under Japanese occupation.

The China Theater was dominated by the Second Sino-Japanese War, a conflict that began in 1937, 4 years before the attack on Pearl Harbor and the outbreak of the Pacific War. The war was characterized by brutality and devastation, with both sides suffering heavy casualties.

▢ *DID YOU KNOW*

- The Second Sino-Japanese War, only ended in 1945, by which time, around 20 million people had died, the majority being Chinese civilians!
- The war resulted in the destruction of half of China, including massive damage to industrial infrastructure and agricultural production.

Japan's invasion of China was met with fierce resistance from Chinese forces, led by the Nationalist government under Chiang Kai-shek and the Communist forces under Mao Zedong. Despite facing a superior enemy, the Chinese people fought with determination, enduring years of hardship and sacrifice to defend their homeland.

The war in China was also marked by atrocities committed by Japanese forces, including the Rape of Nanking, a horrific massacre of Chinese civilians and prisoners of war. These atrocities fueled international condemnation and strengthened the resolve of the Chinese people to resist Japanese aggression.

The U.S. provided financial aid, military equipment, and training to Chinese forces. American volunteer pilots, known as the Flying Tigers, also flew combat missions in support of China, bolstering morale and inflicting losses on Japanese aircraft.

Allied aid was essential for sustaining China's war effort, but it was often hampered by logistical challenges and the difficulty of transporting supplies through Japanese-controlled territory. The Burma Road, a vital supply route linking India to China, was often targeted by Japanese forces, disrupting the flow of aid.

5. Indian Ocean

The Indian Ocean theater, though overshadowed by larger Pacific battles, played a crucial role. It was vital for Allied shipping, connecting the Middle East, India, and Australia, and carrying essential supplies and troops. Protecting these shipping lanes was critical to the Allied war effort in both Europe and Asia.

The Indian Ocean gave Japan the opportunity to disrupt Allied supply lines and threaten British colonies, though its primary focus remained on the Pacific and Southeast Asia. Despite early Japanese naval superiority, British and Allied forces worked to counter Japanese threats and maintain control over the region.

The British Eastern Fleet, based in Colombo, Ceylon (now Sri Lanka), was the primary Allied force in the Indian Ocean. Commanded by Admiral Sir James Somerville, the fleet included battleships, aircraft carriers, cruisers, destroyers, and submarines, with support from Commonwealth nations like Australia, New Zealand, and India. Though initially outmatched, it played a key role in protecting Allied shipping, conducting raids, and supporting operations in Southeast Asia.

Key engagements included the Japanese Raid on Ceylon (April 1942), where Japanese carrier forces attacked British bases, and the Battle of Madagascar (May–November 1942), in which Allied forces seized the island from Vichy France to prevent its use by Japan.

Significance of the Pacific Theater

The Pacific Theater was one of the biggest and most dramatic chapters of World War II. It started with a bang - literally. On December 7, 1941, Japan launched a surprise attack on Pearl Harbor, destroying ships and planes and killing thousands of Americans. This wasn't just an attack on a naval base; it was a declaration of war. Suddenly, the U.S. was all in.

But it wasn't just America in the fight. Japan was on a mission to conquer huge parts of Asia and the Pacific, and they were moving fast. Countries like China, the Philippines, and Australia found themselves under threat or occupation. This was a fight to stop Japan from taking over—and to free the people and places they had already captured.

The Pacific Was the Frontline of a New Kind of War

Unlike the trench warfare of World War I or the tank battles of Europe in World War II, the Pacific Theater was a dynamic mix of naval, air, and land battles, each with its own unique challenges and characteristics. The war here was fought on tiny islands, in dense jungles, and across vast stretches of ocean. Imagine soldiers slogging through knee-deep mud, dodging enemy planes, and storming beaches under heavy fire. It was one of the most grueling and unforgiving theaters of World War II, taking a severe physical and psychological toll.

It wasn't just tough on the ground - it was a showdown of ships and planes, too. This was the war where aircraft carriers became the stars of naval battles. Battles like Midway and Leyte Gulf proved just how powerful air and sea forces could be.

Naval Battles: Carrier Warfare Takes Center Stage

Imagine massive battleships, bristling with guns, exchanging volleys across miles of open ocean. Picture sleek aircraft carriers launching swarms of planes to attack enemy fleets and island bases. Envision submarines lurking beneath the waves, silently stalking their prey and disrupting vital supply lines. This was the naval war in the Pacific, a clash of navies that determined control of the seas and shaped the course of the conflict.

From the surprise attack on Pearl Harbor to the epic Battle of Midway, a turning point that crippled the Japanese fleet, naval battles were crucial in determining the balance of power in the Pacific. These battles involved not only massive warships but also smaller vessels like destroyers, cruisers, and submarines, each playing a vital role in the struggle for supremacy.

The naval war was also a technological race, with both sides constantly developing new weapons and tactics. Radar, sonar, and improved aircraft carriers all played a significant role in the conflict, as did the development of new types of ships, such as the landing craft that enabled amphibious assaults on enemy-held islands.

◻ **DID YOU KNOW**

- Japan developed kaiten, manned torpedoes piloted by suicide crews. These mini-subs were designed to ram into enemy ships, but they had a high failure rate, with many crews dying before reaching their targets.

Air Battles: Dogfights and Strategic Bombing

The skies over the Pacific were also a battleground, with fighter planes engaging in dogfights and bombers raining destruction on enemy targets. From the early days of the war, when Japanese Zero fighters dominated the skies, to the later years, when American Hellcats and Corsairs gained the upper hand, air power played a crucial role.

The development of new aircraft, such as the B-29 Superfortress, which could fly long distances and carry heavy bomb loads, enabled the Allies to strike at the heart of Japan's industrial and military infrastructure.

Air power was also essential for supporting ground troops, providing close air support, disrupting enemy supply lines, and conducting reconnaissance missions.

Land Battles: Jungle Warfare and Island Hopping

The land battles were characterized by two main types of combat: jungle warfare and island hopping. In the dense jungles of Southeast Asia and on many Pacific islands, soldiers faced not only the enemy but also disease, heat, and treacherous terrain. Jungle warfare was grueling and psychologically demanding, requiring soldiers to adapt to challenging conditions and rely on their instincts and training to survive.

Island hopping was a strategy employed by the Allies to capture key islands and use them as bases to advance closer to Japan. While strategically sound, it presented immense challenges. Each island assault was a complex operation, requiring precise coordination between naval, air, and ground forces. The landings were often met with fierce resistance from Japanese defenders entrenched in fortified positions, leading to brutal hand-to-hand combat, intense and bloody battles for control of beaches, airfields, and strategic high ground. The battles for islands like Guadalcanal, Iwo Jima, and Okinawa were some of the most costly and hard-fought of the entire war.

The jungles were another battleground, where soldiers faced not only the enemy but also the harsh realities of nature. The dense vegetation, oppressive heat and humidity, and the constant threat of disease made jungle warfare a grueling and psychologically demanding experience.

Soldiers had to adapt to fighting in an environment where visibility was limited, and ambushes were a constant threat. They learned to navigate treacherous terrain, and endure extreme weather conditions, testing the limits of human endurance and resolve.

The Japanese, with their emphasis on honor and self-sacrifice, fought with a tenacity that often surprised and shocked their American opponents.

☐ **DID YOU KNOW**

- The U.S. used Native American, Navajo Code Talkers in the Pacific. Their language-based code was never broken by the Japanese, making it one of the most effective communication methods of the war.

The Human Cost

The Pacific War was a costly and brutal conflict, with both sides suffering heavy casualties. The fighting was often fierce and unrelenting, with no clear front lines and little respite for the soldiers involved. The war pushed the limits of human endurance and left a lasting mark on those who experienced it.

The human cost of the war was not limited to the battlefield. Civilians were also caught in the crossfire, with cities bombed and entire populations displaced. It left deep scars that would take generations to heal.

Post-War Changes

After its defeat, Japan's empire was dismantled, and the country was occupied by Allied forces, leading to major political and social reforms. The war significantly weakened European colonial powers in Asia, leading to decolonization movements.

The U.S.'s post-war dominance in the Pacific and Asia set the stage for Cold War rivalries, particularly with the Soviet Union and later Communist China.

CHAPTER 2: THE ROAD TO WAR

We've heard about the Pacific War - battleships clashing, fighter planes roaring, and epic island showdowns. But before all the action kicked off, there was a much bigger story unfolding behind the scenes. This chapter is all about what led to the war and Japan's real goals. Spoiler alert: it wasn't just about picking fights for fun.

Picture this: It's the early 20th century, and Japan is rising fast on the world stage. They've gone from an isolated, feudal society to a major industrial and military power in just a few decades. But there's a catch—they're an island nation with few natural resources of their own. To keep growing, Japan needs more land, more power, and, above all, more resources like oil and rubber. Their solution? Expansion. And not just a little bit—they wanted to build a vast empire across Asia and the Pacific.

But Japan wasn't operating in a vacuum. Other countries - China, the United States, Britain, and the European colonial powers - had their own interests in the region. As Japan's ambitions grew, so did the tensions, and it was only a matter of time before the situation exploded into all-out war.

In this chapter, we'll explore why Japan set its sights on domination, how the world reacted (or didn't), and what they were really hoping to achieve. It's a story of big dreams, bold moves, and decisions that changed the course of history.

The Meiji Restoration and Japan's Modernization

In 1868, Japan underwent a dramatic political and social transformation known as the Meiji Restoration. This event marked the end of the feudal Tokugawa shogunate and the restoration of imperial rule under Emperor Meiji. This ushered in an era of modernization and Westernization, as Japan sought to catch up with the industrialized nations of the West.

The government implemented a series of reforms aimed at modernizing Japan's economy, military, and education system. It sent students and officials abroad to study Western technologies and institutions, and it invited foreign experts to Japan to share their knowledge and expertise.

Japan's modernization efforts were remarkably successful. Within a few decades, the country had transformed itself from a largely agrarian society into a major industrial power, with a modern military and a growing economy.

The Rise of Japanese Nationalism

Japan's rapid modernization was accompanied by a surge in nationalism, a sense of pride in its unique culture and achievements. This nationalism was fueled by a desire to assert Japan's place on the world stage and to challenge the dominance of Western powers in Asia.

Japanese nationalism also had a darker side. It was often intertwined with militarism, a belief in the power of the military to achieve national goals. The military played an increasingly important role in Japanese society and politics, and its leaders began to advocate for a more assertive foreign policy, one that would secure Japan's place as the dominant power in Asia.

The Need for Resources and Expansion – "The Greater East Asia Co-Prosperity Sphere"

Japan's rapid industrialization created a growing demand for resources like oil, rubber, and iron ore, which it lacked domestically. To secure these, Japan turned to expansion, targeting resource-rich territories in Asia and the Pacific. This economic drive was coupled with ambitions for national security and prestige, leading to the concept of the Greater East Asia Co-Prosperity Sphere—a bloc of Asian nations under Japanese control, supposedly united for mutual prosperity. However, this was largely propaganda masking imperial ambitions. Rather than liberating Asia from Western rule, Japan exploited conquered territories, extracting resources to fuel its war machine and strengthen its economy.

Japan's expansion began with the Russo-Japanese War (1904–1905), securing Korea and parts of Manchuria. In 1931, Japan invaded Manchuria, establishing the puppet state of Manchukuo, defying international condemnation. In 1937, it launched a full-scale invasion of China, igniting the brutal Second Sino-Japanese War. The occupation saw widespread atrocities, including the Rape of Nanking, further isolating Japan diplomatically.

▢ **DID YOU KNOW**

- The Russo-Japanese War is notable because it marked the first time in modern history that an Asian country had defeated a European country in combat, signifying a shift in global power dynamics.

- The Russo-Japanese War was the first war in which machine guns and trench warfare were used, and that torpedoes were used.

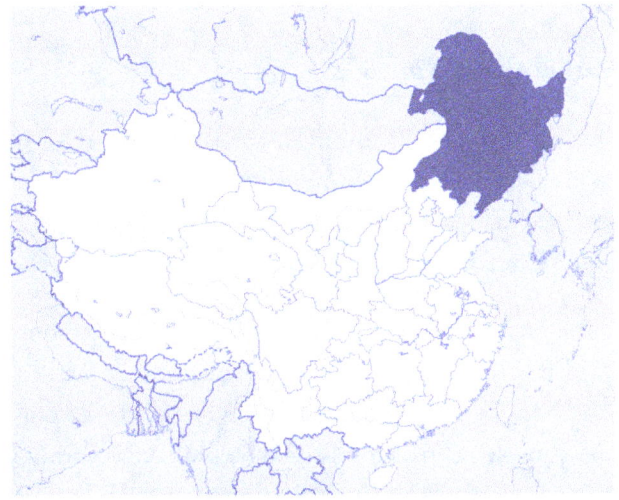

Manchuria, north-east of China

With World War II's outbreak in 1939, Japan seized French Indochina, Malaya, the Dutch East Indies, and the Philippines, securing vital resources. Once in control, Japan imposed strict economic policies, forcing local populations into labor in mines, factories, and plantations. Food shortages, economic collapse, and widespread suffering followed, sparking resistance movements across occupied regions.

The human cost of Japan's empire was immense. Millions suffered forced labor, starvation, disease, and brutality, with atrocities like the Bataan Death March causing widespread devastation. The economic and social damage lasted decades, destabilizing the region. Ultimately, Japan's vision of a Greater East Asia Co-Prosperity Sphere failed, as its conquests led to widespread resistance, Allied retaliation, and its eventual defeat.

Growing Tensions With Other Powers

As Japan flexed its newfound muscles on the world stage, its ambitions inevitably clashed with the interests of other major powers in the region. Japan's desire for expansion and dominance brought it into conflict with established powers. These tensions, simmering beneath the surface, would eventually boil over into a devastating war.

China: A Nation Under Threat

China, with its vast territory and resources, was a prime target for Japan's expansionist ambitions. Japan's invasion of Manchuria in 1931 was met with condemnation from the international community, but Japan, undeterred, continued its encroachment on Chinese sovereignty.

The Second Sino-Japanese War, in 1937, further escalated tensions between the two nations. Japan's brutal occupation of Chinese territory, marked by atrocities like the Rape of Nanking, fueled resentment and resistance among the Chinese people. China's struggle against Japan would become a major front in the Pacific War, drawing in other powers and contributing to the global nature of the conflict.

The United States: A Pacific Power with Growing Concerns

The United States, with its growing economic and strategic interests in the Pacific, watched Japan's expansionism with increasing concern. The U.S. had acquired territories like the Philippines and Guam in the late 19th century, and its trade with Asia was growing rapidly. Japan's ambitions in the region, particularly its encroachment on China, threatened American interests and its vision of an open and stable Pacific.

The U.S. government, initially hesitant to intervene directly, attempted to curb Japan's aggression through diplomatic pressure and economic sanctions. However, these measures proved ineffective, as Japan, driven by its own strategic calculations and a sense of national destiny, continued its expansionist policies.

The tensions between the United States and Japan escalated throughout the 1930s, with Japan's occupation of French Indochina in 1941 proving to be a tipping point in U.S.-Japan relations. The U.S. saw this move as a direct threat to its interests in the region and responded with a decisive economic measure: freezing all Japanese assets in the United States. This effectively cut off Japan's access to American financial markets and severely restricted its ability to purchase vital resources. The United States, Britain, and the Netherlands also cut off Japan's access to oil. At that time, the U.S. supplied 80% of Japan's oil, so cutting off exports had a huge impact on Japan.

The oil embargo was a calculated risk by the U.S. It hoped that the embargo would force Japan to reconsider its aggressive policies and negotiate a peaceful settlement. However, it also carried the risk of pushing Japan into a corner, potentially leading to war.

In an instant, Japan's entire economy and military machine were at risk, with only enough oil reserves to last a year. For Japan's war planners, there was no real choice.

Driven by a combination of national pride, militarism, and a belief in their own destiny, Japan's leaders chose to respond with war.

Great Britain: An Empire Under Pressure

Great Britain, with its vast colonial empire in Asia, also felt threatened by Japan's rise. British colonies like Malaya, Singapore, and Burma were strategically vital for the British Empire, providing resources, trade routes, and military bases. Japan's expansionist ambitions directly challenged British interests and its ability to maintain its colonial holdings.

The fall of Singapore in 1942, a humiliating defeat for the British, exposed the vulnerability of the empire and further fueled tensions with Japan. Britain, already embroiled in a war with Germany and Italy in Europe, found itself stretched thin, struggling to defend its interests in both the European and Pacific theaters.

The European Colonial Powers: A Diminishing Presence

The European colonial powers, such as France and the Netherlands, had significant interests in Asia. France controlled Indochina, while the Netherlands held the Dutch East Indies, both resource-rich territories coveted by Japan.

The war in Europe, however, weakened the European colonial powers, making them vulnerable to Japanese aggression. The fall of France in 1940 created a power vacuum in Indochina, which Japan quickly exploited, occupying the colony and further expanding its influence in Southeast Asia.

The Netherlands, also occupied by Germany, was unable to effectively defend its colonies in the East Indies, which fell to Japan in early 1942. The decline of European colonial powers in Asia created opportunities for Japan's expansionism and contributed to the escalating tensions in the region.

The Road to Pearl Harbor

Japan's expansionist policies and its alliance with Nazi Germany and Italy in 1940 (the Tripartite Pact) further strained its relations with the Western powers. The U.S., witnessing the brutality of Japan's invasion and occupation of China, grew increasingly critical of Japan's actions. President Franklin D. Roosevelt's "Quarantine Speech" in 1937, though not explicitly naming Japan, called for international cooperation to "quarantine" aggressor nations, signaling a shift towards a more assertive U.S. foreign policy.

The U.S. economic sanctions, coupled with Japan's growing frustration with the West and its belief that it could achieve a swift victory, led to the fateful decision to attack Pearl Harbor. The attack, intended to cripple the U.S. Pacific Fleet and buy Japan time to consolidate its conquests, instead galvanized American public opinion and plunged the United States into war.

CHAPTER 3: TIMELINE OF MAJOR EVENTS AND BATTLES

1931–1937: The Build-Up to the Pacific War

- **1931: Japan Invades Manchuria**

    - In September 1931, Japan invades Manchuria, a northeastern region of China, after a staged attack (the Mukden Incident) on a Japanese railway. Japan claims the right to intervene to protect its interests, but the real goal was to control Manchuria's rich resources. Japan set up the puppet state of Manchukuo.

- **1937: Second Sino-Japanese War Begins**

    - On July 7, 1937, the Second Sino-Japanese War officially begins when Japanese forces attack Chinese troops at the Marco Polo Bridge near Beijing. This expanded the Japanese invasion to the whole of China.

- **August 1937: Battle of Shanghai.** One of the longest and most intense battles of the early phase of the war. The Japanese capture Shanghai in November 1937 after fierce fighting, but Chinese forces resist valiantly, inflicting heavy casualties on the Japanese.

- **December 1937:** The Rape of Nanking (Nanjing Massacre). Japanese forces capture Nanjing, the capital of China at the time. During the following six weeks, over 200,000 civilians and prisoners of war are killed, and widespread atrocities, including rape and torture, are committed by the Japanese troops.

1938: War in China continues

- **March 1938: Battle of Tai'erzhuang.** This is a significant Chinese victory in the early part of the war. Chinese forces under General Song Shilun successfully defend the town of Tai'erzhuang in Shandong Province, repelling a Japanese offensive and inflicting heavy casualties on Japan.

- **July 1938: Battle of Wuhan.** Japanese forces advance into central China, attacking the strategic city of Wuhan. The battle lasts for several months, and while Japan ultimately captures Wuhan, it is a costly victory. The Chinese government relocates further inland, continuing to resist.

1939–1940: A Stalemate and Guerrilla Warfare

- **1939–1940: Guerrilla Warfare Intensifies.** As Japanese forces occupy more of China's major cities, Chinese resistance shifts to guerrilla warfare, particularly in the countryside. The Chinese Nationalist forces (under Chiang Kai-shek) and Communist forces (led by Mao Zedong) engage in coordinated resistance efforts, making it difficult for Japan to fully control the vast Chinese territory.

1940: Japan Expands Further in Asia

- **1940: Japan Joins the Axis Powers**

    - In September 1940, Japan signs the Tripartite Pact with Nazi Germany and Fascist Italy, officially joining the Axis Powers in WWII.

    - Japan's expansion into French Indochina (modern-day Vietnam, Laos, and Cambodia) in the same year threatened British and American interests in Asia, escalating tensions in the region.

- **July 1941: Japan Occupies French Indochina**

    - Japan occupies French Indochina to cut off supplies to China and expand its influence in Southeast Asia. This move led the U.S. to impose oil and scrap metal embargos, severely affecting Japan's economy.

- 1941: Battle of Changsha. Japanese forces attempt to capture Changsha, an important city in central China. They fail after heavy resistance from Chinese forces, marking one of Japan's first major setbacks in China.

1941: The U.S. Enters the War

- **December 7, 1941: Attack on Pearl Harbor**

  - Japan launches a surprise attack on the U.S. naval base at Pearl Harbor, Hawaii. Over 2,400 Americans are killed, and eight battleships damaged or sunk.

- **December 8, 1941: The U.S. Declares War on Japan**

  - Following the attack on Pearl Harbor, the United States declares war on Japan. In response, Germany and Italy declare war on the U.S., bringing the U.S. into the European theater as well.

- **December 8, 1941:** Japan attacks American airfields in Luzon, Philippines, destroying 103 aircraft, over half the US air strength. By the end of December, Japan had destroyed all U.S airfields in the Philippines and most of its air power.

- **December 8 - 23, 1941:** Battle of Wake Island, an atoll of 3 coral islets in the central Pacific Ocean, 2,000 miles west of Hawaii. Japan wins the battle, at great cost and holds the Islands until the end of the war.

1942: Early Japanese Successes and First Major Battles

Early 1942 was a disastrous period for the Allied cause in south-east Asia as the Japanese rapidly seized territory

- **January 1942:** Japan captures Guam, Wake Island, the Philippines (including the fall of Bataan and the Bataan Death March), Malaya, New Britain and invades Burma.

- **February 15, 1942: Fall of Singapore.** The British surrender to Japanese forces, marking one of the worst defeats in British military history.

- **February 19, 1942: Darwin, Australia** is hit by a Japanese air raid, the first of 100 such raids.

- **February 27, 1942: Battle of the Java Sea.** Japan defeats the main Allies' naval force, with the Allies losing 5 irreplaceable warships.

- **March 9, 1942: The Dutch East Indies falls** to Japan, after the surrender of the Allies in Java and Sumatra.

- **March-May 1942: Battle of the Coral Sea.** The first major naval battle fought entirely by aircraft carriers. The U.S. and Australia prevent Japan from capturing Port Moresby in New Guinea.

- **April 1, 1942: The Pacific War Council** is formed, to advise on and coordinate the Allied war effort. It includes the U.S. Britain, China, Australia the Netherlands, New Zealand and Canada.

- **April 18, 1942: Doolittle Raid.** The U.S. conducts a daring raid, where 16 B-25 American bombers, led by Lieutenant Colonel James Doolittle, bomb Tokyo and other Japanese cities. While the raid causes minimal damage, it boosts American morale and shows Japan that it is vulnerable to attack. It prompts Japan to divert 4 army fighter groups from the South Pacific to Japan, weakening Japan's attacking forces.

- **April 1942:** Japanese carrier-based aircraft and submarines attack British ships in the Indian Ocean and Bay of Bengal, sinking 30 cargo ships.

- **April 1942:** The Allies divide the Pacific into 2 commands – Douglas

MacArthur is appointed Supreme Commander of SW Pacific including Dutch East Indies, Philippines, Australia the Bismarck Archipelago and the Solomons. The Pacific Ocean command is given to Chester Nimitz. They have near identical missions: to hold the line of communications between the United States and Australia; to contain the Japanese within the Pacific; to support the defense of North America; and to prepare for major amphibious counteroffensives.

- **May 6 – 31, 1942: Battle of Salween River.** Japan launches an offensive against Chinese forces along the Salween River (in modern-day Myanmar). This marks the beginning of Japan's push into the southwest of China. The battle is part of a larger effort to secure supply routes through Burma to China, and it marks a shift in the strategic direction of the conflict.

- **May 1942: Japan captures Burma** and the British retreat to India

- **June 3 - 7, 1942: Battle of Midway.** In one of the most important turning points in the Pacific War, the United States, using cryptography to decode Japanese messages, ambushes the Japanese fleet near Midway Atoll. The U.S. sinks four Japanese aircraft carriers, and kills most of its best-trained naval pilots, dealing a devastating blow to Japan's naval power and shifting the balance of power in the Pacific. As a result, Japan abandons plans to invade Samoa, New Caledonia and Fiji.

- **June 8, 1942**: 2 Japanese submarines shell Sydney's eastern suburbs.

- **August 7, 1942 - February 9, 1943: Battle of Guadalcanal** – The first major Allied offensive in the Pacific. U.S. forces defeat Japanese troops, marking the start of the "island-hopping" campaign.

1943 - 1944: Turning the Tide Against Japan

After Midway, the U.S. began to harness its vast industrial potential to greatly increase production of ships, planes, and other materiel, and to train more airmen at an increasing rate.

After its loss in the Battle of Guadalcanal, the Japanese adopted a defensive strategy, focusing on strengthening its remaining defensive positions while launching counterattacks where it could.

The Allies began a protracted Island-Hopping campaign across the Pacific Theater, seizing several island bases in a series of (often bloody) amphibious assaults against determined Japanese defenders.

- **February 1943: Guadalcanal Campaign Ends.** After six months of brutal fighting in the Solomon Islands, the U.S. achieves its first major victory over Japan in the Guadalcanal Campaign. This marks the beginning of the U.S. strategy of island-hopping, bypassing heavily fortified Japanese positions and capturing key islands to move closer to Japan.

- **March 2 – 4, 1943:** U.S. and Australian forces achieve victory in the Battle of the Bismarck Sea, sinking a Japanese convoy. This prevents the Japanese from gaining a presence in Papua and New Guinea, Australia's nearest neighbour.

- **April 18, 1943:** Marshal Admiral Yamamoto Isoroku, commander-in-chief of the Japanese Combined Fleet and one of the supporters of the attack on Pearl Harbour, is killed in an ambush by U.S. fighters when he and his staff were flying from Rabaul to Buin. His death was a significant blow to the Japanese Navy.

- **May 11, 1943:** US troops land on Attu in the Aleutian Islands, southeast of Alaska. This prevents further Japanese attacks on the U.S. mainland and also leads the Japanese to fear a U.S. invasion from the Aleutians.

- **June 1943: Operation Cartwheel** begins, with Allied forces pushing Japanese forces out of the Solomon Islands, the Gilbert Islands, and parts of New Guinea.

- **November 1943: Battle of Changde.** Major battle of the 2nd Sino-Japan War around the city of Changde. This battle saw the Japanese use chemical weapons.

- **November 20-23, 1943: Battle of Tarawa.** U.S. forces capture the heavily fortified Japanese island of Tarawa in the Gilbert Islands, but at a high cost.

- **1944: Battle of Zaoyang-Yichang.** Japanese forces try to secure control over central China, particularly in the Hubei and Hunan provinces. Despite the Japanese numerical advantage, the Chinese forces inflict heavy casualties on the Japanese, marking a key point in the larger struggle.

- **1944: Battle of Hengyang.** Japan launches an attempt to capture the city of Hengyang in southern China. The Chinese defenders put up fierce resistance, forcing the Japanese to withdraw and signaling the beginning of a long period of attrition for Japan.

- **June 15 - July 9, 1944: Battle of Saipan.** A key victory for the Allies, capturing the island from Japan. This also brought the U.S. within bombing range of Japan.

- **October 23-26, 1944: Battle of Leyte Gulf.** One of the largest naval battles in history, the U.S. Navy decisively defeats the Japanese fleet, securing control of the Philippines.

- **October 1944:** The U.S. begins the campaign to liberate the Philippines, which has been under Japanese occupation since 1942. The successful Battle of Leyte in October 1944 marks the beginning of the liberation of the Philippines.

1945: The Final Push Toward Japan, and its surrender

- **February 19 - March 26, 1945: Battle of Iwo Jima.** U.S. Marines capture the island of Iwo Jima after a grueling battle. The iconic image of U.S. soldiers raising the American flag on Mount Suribachi becomes a symbol of the Pacific War.

- **January–March 1945: The Battle of Changde.** Japanese forces attempt to capture Changde in the Hunan Province, but the Chinese defenders manage to hold out, forcing Japan into a costly retreat.

- **April 1 - June 22, 1945: Battle of Okinawa.** The last major battle, and one of the bloodiest, of the Pacific War, where U.S. forces capture the Japanese island of Okinawa. The battle results in massive casualties on both sides and provides a staging area for a potential invasion of Japan.

- **May 1942: Allies recapture Burma**

- **July 16, 1945: First Atomic Bomb Test** at the Trinity site in New Mexico.

- **August 6, 1945: The U.S. drops the first atomic bomb on Hiroshima, Japan.**

- **August 9, 1945: The U.S. drops the second atomic bomb on Nagasaki.** The bombings caused immense destruction and death, leading Japan to realize that continued resistance is futile.

- **August 15, 1945: Japan announces its surrender.** Emperor Hirohito announces Japan's surrender on the radio, effectively ending the war.

- **September 2, 1945: Formal surrender.** Japan signs the formal instrument of surrender aboard the USS Missouri in Tokyo Bay, officially ending WWII.

Post-War Events

- **September 1945:** The U.S. begins the occupation of Japan, led by General Douglas MacArthur, marking the start of a long process of demilitarization and rebuilding.

- **1947:** The Japanese Constitution is adopted, formally ending Japan's military power and establishing a pacifist government.

CHAPTER 4: WAR PLANS

Japan's Strategy in World War II

Pre-War Planning

Japan's entry into World War II was not a sudden, impulsive decision. It was the culmination of years of meticulous planning, driven by a complex web of strategic goals and calculations. In the years leading up to the war, Japanese military leaders and policymakers carefully crafted a strategy aimed at achieving quick and decisive victories, securing vital resources, and establishing Japan as the dominant power in Asia and the Pacific.

Let's explore the key elements of Japan's pre-war planning, highlighting the strategic thinking, alliances, and miscalculations that shaped its path to war.

The Quest for Quick and Decisive Victories

Japan's pre-war strategy was heavily influenced by its experience in previous conflicts, particularly the Russo-Japanese War of 1904-1905. In that war, Japan had achieved a stunning victory against Russia, a major European power, through a series of swift and decisive military campaigns. This experience instilled in Japanese military leaders a belief in the importance of achieving quick and decisive victories to secure strategic objectives and demoralize the enemy.

This emphasis on speed and decisiveness was reflected in Japan's pre-war planning for World War II. The military envisioned a series of rapid offensives aimed at capturing key territories and resources before the Allied powers, particularly the United States, could effectively respond. This strategy relied on a combination of surprise attacks, lightning-fast advances, and the exploitation of perceived weaknesses in Allied defenses.

The Role of Alliances: The Axis Powers

Japan's pre-war planning involved forging alliances with other expansionist powers. In 1940, Japan signed the Tripartite Pact with Nazi Germany and Fascist

Italy, formally joining the Axis powers. This alliance was seen as a way to deter potential adversaries, particularly the United States, from intervening in Japan's expansionist ambitions.

The alliance with the Axis powers, however, also carried risks. It tied Japan's fate to that of its European allies, whose war against Britain and its allies was far from certain. Moreover, the alliance with Nazi Germany, with its abhorrent ideology of racial supremacy, would ultimately tarnish Japan's image and complicate its relations with the Western powers after the war.

The Focus on Naval Power

Japan's placed a strong emphasis on naval power. The Imperial Japanese Navy (IJN) was seen as the key to achieving Japan's strategic goals. The IJN had undergone a significant modernization and expansion in the years leading up to the war, and its leaders were confident in their ability to dominate the seas and project power across the region.

The IJN's pre-war planning focused on developing a powerful carrier force, capable of launching devastating air strikes against enemy fleets and land targets. The attack on Pearl Harbor was a reflection of the IJN's carrier warfare ability and its belief in the importance of achieving surprise and decisiveness in naval combat.

The Underestimation of the United States

One of the most significant miscalculations in Japan's pre-war planning was its underestimation of the United States. Japanese leaders believed the U.S., facing strong isolationist sentiments at home, would be reluctant to engage in a protracted war in the Pacific.

They also underestimated the industrial and military might of the United States. They believed that Japan could achieve a quick victory in Southeast Asia before the U.S. could mobilize its full strength. However, the U.S., with its vast industrial capacity and technological prowess, quickly ramped up its war production and deployed its forces to the Pacific, turning the tide of the war in its favor.

The attack on Pearl Harbor, intended to be a decisive blow against the U.S. Pacific Fleet, instead galvanized the American people and unified them in their determination to defeat Japan.

Early War Strategy

Japan's early war strategy was a bold and ambitious gamble, characterized by a series of swift and decisive offensives aimed at achieving surprise, capturing vital territories, and establishing a dominant position in Asia and the Pacific.

Surprise and Rapid Expansion: The Initial Onslaught

Japan's early war strategy was predicated on the element of surprise. The attack on Pearl Harbor was a carefully planned and executed operation aimed at crippling the U.S. Pacific Fleet and preventing it from interfering with Japan's conquest of Southeast Asia.

This was followed by a series of rapid offensives across the Pacific and Southeast Asia. Japanese forces, employing a combination of superior tactics, air power, and naval dominance, quickly overran Allied defenses, capturing key territories and securing vital resources.

Simultaneous Campaigns: A Multi-Pronged Offensive

Japan launched simultaneous campaigns on multiple fronts, stretching Allied forces thin and preventing them from concentrating their defenses. This multi-pronged offensive aimed to overwhelm the Allies and secure control of key territories before they could effectively respond.

The simultaneous campaigns targeted a wide range of Allied territories, including:

- **The Philippines:** To eliminate the U.S. military presence in Asia and secure a strategic foothold in Southeast Asia.

- **Malaya and Singapore:** To neutralize British power and secure access to vital resources, such as rubber and tin.

- **The Dutch East Indies (Indonesia):** To secure oil resources, crucial for sustaining Japan's war effort.

- **Hong Kong, Burma, and Guam:** To control key trade routes and establish defensive perimeters.

This multi-pronged offensive, while initially successful, ultimately overstretched Japan's resources and led to logistical challenges that would hinder its war effort in the long run.

Naval Dominance: The Key to Victory

Japan relied heavily on its naval dominance. The IJN, with its powerful carrier force and experienced pilots, was considered the key to achieving Japan's strategic goals in the Pacific and Southeast Asia.

The IJN's early victories, such as the Battle of the Coral Sea, demonstrated its ability to project power across vast distances and inflict heavy losses on Allied forces. However, these victories also exposed Japan's vulnerabilities, particularly its reliance on its carrier force and its limited ability to replace lost ships and experienced personnel.

The Limits of Early Success

While initially successful, Japan's early war strategy ultimately proved unsustainable. The rapid expansion of its empire overstretched its resources and led to logistical challenges that hindered its ability to maintain its offensive momentum.

The Allies, particularly the United States, quickly mobilized their industrial and military might, turning the tide of the war in their favor. The Battle of Midway in June 1942 marked a decisive turning point, as the U.S. Navy crippled Japan's carrier force and inflicted heavy losses on its experienced pilots.

Mid-War Adjustments

Japan's initial strategy of swift and decisive victories faltered as the tide began to turn against them in 1942. Its defeat at Midway forced Japan to reassess its strategic approach and adapt to the changing realities of the war. This mid-war adjustment involved a shift towards a more defensive posture, focusing on consolidating its gains, establishing a defensive perimeter, and employing guerrilla warfare tactics in China to drain Allied resources and prolong the conflict.

From Offense to Defense: A Strategic Shift

The loss of four aircraft carriers and hundreds of experienced pilots at Midway severely weakened Japan's naval power and shattered its illusion of invincibility. It forced Japan to abandon its strategy of rapid expansion and adopt a more defensive posture.

This strategic shift was a difficult pill to swallow for Japan's military leaders, who had been accustomed to victories and territorial gains. However, the realities of the war, particularly the growing industrial and military might of the United States, forced them to acknowledge the need for a new approach.

Establishing a Defensive Perimeter: Holding the Line

Japan's new strategy focused on consolidating its gains and establishing a defensive perimeter to protect its home islands and newly conquered territories. This perimeter, stretching across the vast expanse of the Pacific Ocean and Southeast Asia, was intended to deter Allied advances and inflict heavy casualties, potentially forcing a negotiated peace.

The defensive perimeter consisted of a network of fortified islands, airbases, and naval bases, strategically positioned to create a layered defense system. Japan invested heavily in fortifying these positions, constructing bunkers, tunnels, and other defensive structures designed to withstand Allied attacks.

This defensive strategy, while strategically sound, faced significant challenges. The vast expanse of the perimeter strained Japan's resources and logistics, making it difficult to defend every position effectively. Moreover, the Allies' island-hopping campaign, which bypassed heavily fortified islands and focused on capturing strategically vital ones, gradually eroded Japan's defensive perimeter.

Guerrilla Warfare in China: Draining Allied Resources

In China, Japan shifted towards guerrilla warfare tactics. The Japanese military, facing a protracted and costly conflict against both Nationalist and Communist forces, sought to drain Allied resources and prolong the war, hoping to force a negotiated settlement that would preserve its gains in China.

Japanese forces adopted a strategy of attrition, employing hit-and-run tactics, ambushes, and sabotage to harass Chinese forces and disrupt their operations. They also sought to exploit the political divisions between the Nationalists and Communists, hoping to weaken their resistance and create opportunities for Japanese advances.

While effective in some areas, the strategy ultimately failed. The Chinese resistance, fueled by nationalism and a determination to liberate their homeland, continued to grow stronger. The Allies, particularly the United States, also increased their support for China, providing financial aid, military equipment, and training to Chinese forces.

The Human Cost of the Mid-War Strategy

Japan's strategy, while intended to prolong the war and force a negotiated peace, came at a heavy human cost. The battles for the defensive perimeter were often brutal and costly, with heavy casualties on both sides. The guerrilla warfare in China resulted in widespread suffering and destruction, as Japanese forces often resorted to scorched-earth tactics and reprisals against civilian populations.

The war also took a heavy toll on the Japanese home front. The Allied blockade of Japan's ports disrupted its economy and led to food shortages and rationing. The strategic bombing campaign, launched from captured islands in the Marianas, inflicted heavy damage on Japan's cities and industrial centers, causing widespread civilian casualties.

Late-War Strategy

By 1944, the tide of the Pacific War had decisively turned against Japan. The once seemingly invincible Japanese military machine was now reeling from a series of defeats, dwindling resources, and a collapsing home front. Yet, despite the grim reality, Japan's leaders refused to surrender, clinging to a desperate hope of reversing their fortunes or at least securing a more favorable peace settlement. This defiance led to a dramatic shift in Japan's late-war strategy, characterized by increasingly desperate measures, including kamikaze attacks, a tenacious defense of key islands, and the mobilization of the entire nation for a final, all-out resistance.

Kamikaze Tactics: A Weapon of Despair

As the Allied forces closed in on the Japanese home islands, Japan's military leaders, facing a shortage of experienced pilots and dwindling aircraft, resorted to a desperate tactic: kamikaze attacks. Kamikaze, meaning "divine wind," (named after the legendary typhoons that saved Japan from Mongol invasions in the 13th century) referred to suicide attacks in which Japanese pilots deliberately crashed their planes into Allied ships, sacrificing their lives in the hope of inflicting maximum damage and demoralizing the enemy.

Japanese kamikaze pilots before battle.

The first organized kamikaze attacks were launched during the Battle of Leyte Gulf in October 1944. These attacks, while shocking and initially effective, ultimately failed to prevent the Allied victory. However, the use of kamikaze tactics escalated in the final months of the war, as Japan's situation grew increasingly desperate.

Kamikaze pilots, often young and inexperienced, were indoctrinated with a sense of patriotic duty and self-sacrifice. They were promised a glorious death and eternal honor for their willingness to give their lives for the emperor and the nation. The psychological impact of these attacks on Allied sailors was significant, but the kamikaze ultimately failed to alter the course of the war.

Island Defense: A Tenacious Last Stand

Japan's focused on a tenacious defense of key islands, particularly Iwo Jima and Okinawa, which were seen as the last line of defense before the Japanese home islands. The battles for these islands were among the bloodiest of the entire war, as Japanese soldiers, entrenched in fortified positions and caves, fought with fanatical resistance, often to the last man.

The Battle of Iwo Jima, fought in February and March 1945, was a particularly brutal and costly struggle. The island, a volcanic fortress with a network of underground tunnels and bunkers, was defended by Japanese forces determined to inflict maximum casualties on the U.S. Marines tasked with capturing it.

The Battle of Okinawa, fought from April to June 1945, was even more costly and protracted. The island, located just 350 miles from the Japanese home islands, was strategically vital for the Allies, as it provided a staging ground for a potential invasion of Japan.

The Japanese defenders fought with a ferocity that shocked and demoralized Allied forces.

Total War: Mobilizing the Nation

As the war entered its final stages, Japan's leaders declared a policy of "total war," mobilizing the entire nation for a final, all-out resistance against the Allied invasion that they believed was imminent. This policy involved the conscription of civilians, including women and children, into the war effort, the arming of civilians with makeshift weapons, and the preparation of the home islands for a bloody and protracted defense.

The total war policy reflected the desperation of Japan's leaders and their unwillingness to accept defeat. They believed that by inflicting heavy casualties on the Allies, they could force them to negotiate a more favorable peace settlement that would preserve Japan's sovereignty and its imperial system.

America's War Plans: From Defense to Counterattack

Before the attack on Pearl Harbor, the United States had been preparing for war, but not expecting it so soon. The U.S. military leadership had devised a series of strategic plans in case war with Japan broke out.

War Plan Orange: The Original Strategy

Since the early 1900s, U.S. military planners had been anticipating a war with Japan. Their strategy, known as War Plan Orange, was based on the assumption that Japan would strike first, the Philippines would fall quickly, and that the U.S. Navy would have to fight its way across the Pacific to reclaim lost territory.

The plan called for a gradual island-hopping campaign, pushing Japanese forces back one step at a time. However, after Pearl Harbor, the situation changed dramatically.

Defensive Posture: Holding the Line

With much of the U.S. Pacific Fleet crippled, the first priority was defense. Hawaii and the U.S. West Coast were fortified against potential Japanese attacks. Australia became a key Allied base, a launching point for future counterattacks. Aircraft carriers became the new focus, replacing battleships as the dominant force in naval warfare.

Though Japan had won the opening battles, the U.S. was already planning its counteroffensive.

Turning the Tide: America's New Strategy

By mid-1942, the United States had recovered from Pearl Harbor. Now, the focus shifted to going on the offensive.

This offensive attitude began with The Doolittle Raid of April 18, 1942, when the U.S. launched a daring bombing raid on Tokyo. Though the attack caused minimal damage, it sent a powerful message that Japan was not invincible, and that the U.S. could strike back. As a consequence, morale soared among American troops and civilians.

This was the first step toward shifting the momentum of the war.

Japan, believing the U.S. was still weak, launched an attack on Midway Atoll (June 4-7, 1942), hoping to destroy the remaining U.S. aircraft carriers.

However, U.S. codebreakers intercepted Japanese communications and set up an ambush.

Four Japanese aircraft carriers were sunk, and its ability to launch further offensives was crippled.

From this point forward, Japan was on the defensive.

The Island-Hopping Campaign: America's Strategy to Crush Japan

With momentum shifting, the U.S. adopted its island-hopping strategy. Instead of attacking every Japanese-held island, the U.S. would target key strategic locations. Bypassed islands were cut off and left to wither, depriving Japan of vital supply lines. Major battles at Guadalcanal, Tarawa, and the Philippines slowly pushed Japan back.

This method was effective but costly. The U.S. suffered heavy casualties, and Japanese forces fought to the death rather than surrender.

The Battle for the Pacific Begins

The war plans of both Japan and the United States set the course of history. Japan's attack-first strategy gave it an early advantage, but overstretched its resources. America's defensive posture allowed it to recover, adapt, and eventually take the offensive. The conflict that began with Pearl Harbor and rapid Japanese expansion would end with atomic bombs falling on Hiroshima and Nagasaki in 1945.

What began as a calculated gamble for resources turned into a brutal war that shaped the modern world.

CHAPTER 5: THE BRUTAL REALITY OF THE PACIFIC WAR

The Pacific War was a theater of extremes, pushing the limits of human endurance in a battleground unlike any other. The terrain, extreme weather, the psychological impact of savage fighting, and disease all played a part in making this a brutal war.

The Terrain: An Unforgiving Environment

The unforgiving terrain of the Pacific Theater shaped the war's brutality, influencing tactics and testing the endurance of soldiers. From dense jungles to rugged mountains and isolated islands, the landscape itself became a formidable enemy.

Jungle Warfare

Imagine a battlefield where the enemy is hidden in a thick, green maze, where every step could trigger a deadly ambush, and where the oppressive heat and humidity sap your strength and will. This was the reality of jungle warfare in the Pacific.

Thick vegetation turned battlefields into nightmarish mazes, where hidden enemies, oppressive heat, and disease created an unrelenting struggle. Limited visibility heightened fear, while insects, humidity, and poor sanitation drained morale. Soldiers had to rely on stealth, adaptability, and sheer endurance to survive in these grueling conditions.

Mountain Warfare

Steep, jungle-clad mountains - such as those in New Guinea and Guadalcanal—posed immense challenges. Treacherous trails, harsh weather, and the lack of infrastructure made movement and supply lines difficult. Japanese forces fortified mountainsides with bunkers and tunnels, forcing Allied troops into costly, brutal assaults.

Island Warfare

Scattered across vast ocean expanses, isolated islands became battlefields for some of the war's fiercest combat. Amphibious landings were met with heavy resistance from well-entrenched defenders, while Japanese garrisons, often cut off from reinforcements, fought to the last man. Battles like Iwo Jima and Okinawa saw staggering casualties, with soldiers locked in close-quarters, relentless combat.

The Human Toll

The Pacific terrain contributed to high casualty rates and unimaginable suffering. Whether navigating the dense jungle, scaling rugged peaks, or storming remote islands, soldiers faced a brutal, inch-by-inch fight for survival. The landscape didn't just shape the war—it defined its intensity and horror.

Extreme Weather: A Relentless Adversary

Battles were fought in some of the most extreme weather conditions on Earth, from sweltering heat and monsoon rains to devastating typhoons. These elements intensified the hardship of battle, testing endurance and complicating operations.

Tropical Heat and Humidity

Imagine fighting a war in a sauna, where the air is thick with moisture, your clothes are constantly soaked with sweat, and every movement feels like an immense effort. This was the reality for soldiers fighting in the tropical regions of the Pacific, where the combination of high temperatures and humidity created a stifling and oppressive environment.

The oppressive heat and humidity drained soldiers' strength, leading to dehydration, heat exhaustion, and rampant disease. Malaria, dengue fever, and dysentery spread rapidly, weakening entire units. Equipment also suffered - guns jammed, tanks overheated, and radios malfunctioned. Even basic tasks, like digging trenches or carrying supplies, became exhausting ordeals.

Monsoon Rains: Turning Battlefields into Quagmires

Torrential monsoons flooded trenches, washed away roads, and bogged down supply lines. Thick mud trapped vehicles and made movement treacherous. Disease-carrying insects thrived, worsening the already dire conditions. Air operations were grounded, limiting vital support. The rains often gave an advantage to defenders, particularly the Japanese, who used the conditions for surprise attacks and ambushes.

Typhoons: Nature's Fury

Powerful typhoons wreaked havoc, sinking ships, crippling bases, and disrupting operations. One of the most devastating was Typhoon Cobra (December 1944), which struck the U.S. Third Fleet, sinking three destroyers and killing over 700 sailors.

Psychological Strain

Soldiers on both sides faced immense psychological challenges, from the fear of the unknown and fanatical resistance to suicidal attacks, exhaustion, and isolation. These mental burdens were as devastating as physical wounds.

Fear of the Unknown: An Invisible Enemy

Imagine fighting an enemy you can't see, hidden in the shadows of the jungle or the depths of a cave, waiting to strike at any moment. This was the reality for many soldiers in the Pacific, where the Japanese often employed guerrilla tactics, ambushes, and surprise attacks. The fear of the unknown, the constant anticipation of danger lurking around every corner, created a pervasive sense of anxiety and dread that weighed heavily on the soldiers' minds.

Fear of capture added to the strain, as Japanese forces were notorious for brutal treatment of prisoners of war.

Fanatical Resistance: Facing an Unflinching Enemy

The Japanese, influenced by the Bushido code, refused to surrender. The banzai charge, a suicidal frontal assault often launched at night, was a terrifying tactic.

The sight and sound of hundreds of Japanese soldiers charging into machine-gun fire, screaming "banzai" (ten thousand years), was a chilling experience that left a lasting impression on those who witnessed it.

The traditional notion of surrender as an honorable option was absent in the Japanese military culture, creating a psychological barrier that made it difficult for Allied soldiers to understand and predict their enemy's behavior.

Key battles demonstrated this:

- **Saipan (1944):** 4,000 Japanese launched the largest banzai charge of the war. Even civilians, fearing American torture, committed mass suicide by leaping off cliffs.

- **Iwo Jima (1945):** Out of 21,000 Japanese defenders, only 216 surrendered. Many fought with bayonets and fists when out of ammunition.

- **Okinawa (1945):** Over 100,000 Japanese soldiers and civilians perished, many choosing suicide over capture. Kamikaze pilots launched mass suicide attacks on U.S. warships.

Kamikaze Attacks: The Ultimate Psychological Weapon

In desperation, Japan introduced kamikaze attacks, the suicide bombing of Allied ships. Though not always effective, they inflicted damage and, more importantly, instilled fear. Watching an enemy deliberately sacrifice themselves created an overwhelming sense of vulnerability and dread.

Exhaustion and Isolation: The Wear and Tear of War

The Pacific War was relentless. Soldiers endured prolonged battles with little rest, extreme weather, and harsh terrain. Sleep deprivation, constant danger, and isolation eroded morale, making survival as much a mental battle as a physical one.

The Brutality of Combat

Fighting was brutal, and unforgiving, with soldiers on both sides facing a level of violence and savagery that left deep physical and psychological scars.

Close-Quarters Fighting: No Room for Mercy

The dense jungles, rugged mountains, and confined island battlefields forced soldiers into savage, hand-to-hand combat. In places like Guadalcanal and New Guinea, soldiers fought with bayonets, knives, and even bare hands in chaotic, life-or-death struggles. On Iwo Jima and Okinawa, Japanese defenders, entrenched in tunnels and caves, fought with relentless tenacity, making every inch of ground a hard-won victory.

High Casualties: The Heavy Price of War

The Pacific War's relentless nature led to staggering losses:

- **Guadalcanal (1942-43):** 7,000 Americans and over 20,000 Japanese killed.

- **Iwo Jima (1945):** Nearly 7,000 U.S. Marines and over 20,000 Japanese defenders killed.

- **Okinawa (1945):** The costliest battle, with 12,000 U.S. troops killed, 50,000 wounded, and 100,000 Japanese soldiers dead.

Civilians: The Unintended Victims

Civilians endured immense suffering. Under Japanese occupation, forced labor, executions, and atrocities like the Rape of Nanking showcased the war's brutality. Allied bombing campaigns were equally devastating:

- **Tokyo Firebombing (March 1945):** 100,000 killed, 25% of the city destroyed.

- **Atomic Bombings (August 1945):** Hiroshima and Nagasaki suffered unprecedented destruction, with tens of thousands instantly killed and many more suffering long-term radiation effects.

Disease and Starvation: The Silent Killers

Beyond combat, disease and starvation ravaged soldiers and civilians alike, fueled by the tropical environment, poor sanitation, and logistical struggles.

Malaria: The Invisible Enemy

Mosquito-infested jungles made malaria a relentless threat. Fevers, chills, and exhaustion incapacitated soldiers for weeks, reducing combat effectiveness. Despite efforts like quinine and mosquito nets, the disease claimed countless casualties, particularly among ill-equipped Japanese troops.

Dysentery: A Crippling Affliction

Unsanitary conditions and contaminated water led to dysentery, causing severe diarrhea, dehydration, and rapid deterioration. In the sweltering heat, dehydration could be fatal, and limited medical supplies only worsened the crisis.

Skin Infections: The Unrelenting Nuisance

Constant exposure to heat, humidity, and moisture led to fungal infections, rashes, and ulcers, making daily life miserable. Left untreated, these infections could worsen, further weakening soldiers.

Starvation: The Slow and Cruel Killer

As Allied blockades cut off Japanese supply lines, starvation became widespread. Isolated troops resorted to eating insects, plants, and even the flesh of fallen comrades. Hunger weakened bodies, eroded morale, and increased vulnerability to disease.

Civilians also suffered, as Japan diverted resources to its military, causing famine and malnutrition across occupied territories, particularly in China and Southeast Asia.

Disease and starvation were just as deadly as bullets, turning survival itself into a daily battle.

◻ **DID YOU KNOW**

- *Tropical diseases like malaria, dysentery, and beriberi killed more Japanese soldiers than actual battle wounds. The lack of medical supplies and harsh jungle conditions made survival nearly impossible.*

CHAPTER 6: MAPS OF THE PACIFIC CAMPAIGN

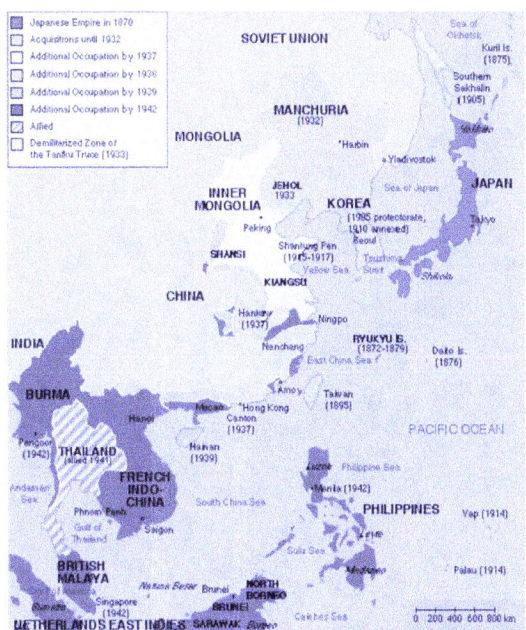

Map of Japanese held territory pre-WW2 and to 1942

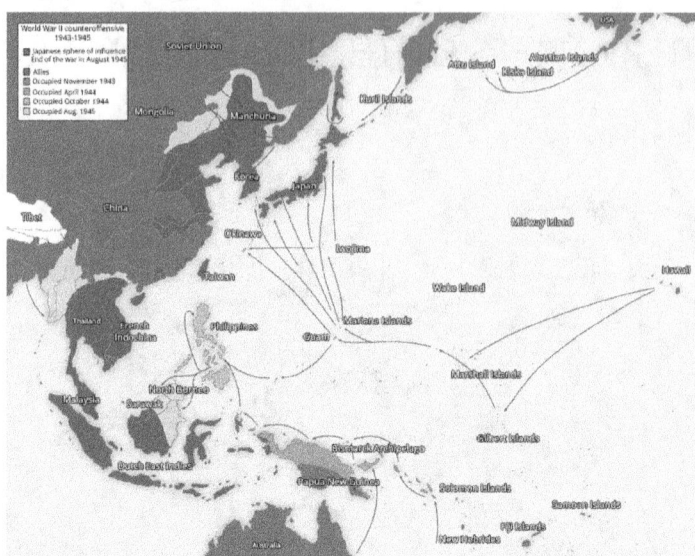

Map of The United States' Island-Hopping Campaign, World War 2

CHAPTER 7: KEY LEADERS AND GENERALS

The Pacific War was shaped not only by the brutal battles fought across vast oceans and unforgiving jungles but also by the commanders who orchestrated them. These leaders made decisions that shaped the course of history. Some were revered, others feared, but all played a crucial role in one of the most intense conflicts the world has ever seen. Let's explore the minds, tactics, and legacies of the men who led their nations through the fires of war.

Allied Leaders

General Douglas MacArthur: The "American Caesar"

A towering figure in the Pacific War, General MacArthur was known for his charisma, bold strategy, and dramatic flair. A World War I veteran and Medal of Honor recipient, he became Supreme Commander of Allied Forces in the Southwest Pacific in 1942.

General Douglas MacArthur

MacArthur's leadership combined confidence and public relations mastery - his famous vow, "I shall return," after the fall of the Philippines, inspired both troops and the American public. His strategy centered on reclaiming the Philippines, leading successful campaigns across New Guinea, the Solomons, and Manila in 1945.

His legacy remains complex - praised for his courage and leadership, yet criticized for ego, defiance of authority, and pursuit of personal glory.

▫ **DID YOU KNOW**

- *MacArthur accepted the surrender of Japan on September 2, 1945.*

- *He ran for the Republican Party's presidential nomination in 1952 but lost to Dwight Eisenhower.*

Admiral Chester W. Nimitz: The Master Strategist

As Commander in Chief of the U.S. Pacific Fleet, Admiral Nimitz orchestrated key naval victories, including Midway, Guadalcanal, and the Mariana Islands campaign. A skilled strategist and logistics expert, he played a pivotal role in the Pacific War.

Admiral Chester W. Nimitz

Unlike MacArthur's flamboyance, Nimitz led with calm precision, basing decisions on intelligence and meticulous planning. He championed the island-hopping strategy, systematically weakening Japan's naval power and paving the way for victory.

Nimitz's legacy is one of strategic brilliance and quiet resolve, his leadership proving essential to the Allied success in the Pacific.

◻ **DID YOU KNOW**

- *Nimitz's greatest legacy as Chief of Naval Operations is arguably his support of Admiral Hyman Rickover's effort to convert the submarine fleet from diesel to nuclear propulsion.*

Admiral William "Bull" Halsey Jr.: The Aggressive Commander

A bold and relentless commander, Admiral Halsey led the Third Fleet with an offensive spirit that defined his leadership. Key to victories in the Solomon Islands campaign and the Battle of Leyte Gulf, he was known for his risk-taking tactics and eagerness to engage the enemy.

Admiral William "Bull" Halsey Jr

While his aggression often paid off, it also led to setbacks, such as being lured away at Leyte Gulf by a Japanese decoy force. Yet, Halsey's courage and determination made him a respected leader, leaving a legacy of boldness and unyielding warfare.

General Joseph "Vinegar Joe" Stilwell: The China-Burma-India Commander

A tough and outspoken leader, General Stilwell commanded U.S. and Chinese forces in the China-Burma-India Theater (CBI), tasked with supporting China's resistance and securing new supply routes. His mission was hindered by logistical struggles, political tensions, and the challenging terrain of the region.

General Joseph "Vinegar Joe" Stilwell

Stilwell's blunt personality led to frequent clashes with Chiang Kai-shek, frustrating efforts to coordinate the war effort. Despite setbacks, he oversaw the construction of the Ledo Road, a vital supply route. However, his deteriorating relationship with Chiang led to his recall in 1944.

Stilwell's legacy is one of determination and controversy - a skilled strategist whose abrasive style ultimately limited his influence.

☐ **DID YOU KNOW**

- *He earned his nickname from a caricature of himself rising from a vinegar bottle. A subordinate drew the cartoon after Stilwell criticized their performance in a field exercise.*

General Holland M. "Howlin' Mad" Smith: The Father of Modern Amphibious Warfare

A pioneer of amphibious warfare, General Smith played a key role in the island-hopping strategy, commanding Marine forces in Tarawa, Saipan, and Iwo

Jima. A demanding but respected leader, he emphasized rigorous training and meticulous planning, ensuring his troops were prepared for brutal assaults.

Smith revolutionized amphibious warfare, developing new tactics and equipment that proved vital to the Pacific campaign. His legacy as the "father of modern amphibious warfare" remains a cornerstone of military strategy today.

◻ **DID YOU KNOW**

- *Smith earned his nickname due to his fiery temper, outspoken nature, and aggressive leadership style.*

Admiral Raymond A. Spruance: The Quiet Strategist

Admiral Spruance was a brilliant strategist and decisive leader, known for his calm, analytical mind and adaptability under pressure. As commander of the Fifth Fleet, he played a key role in victories at Midway and the Philippine Sea.

A meticulous planner, Spruance emphasized carrier warfare and maintaining the initiative against Japan. His leadership at Midway, where he made bold yet calculated decisions, was instrumental in turning the tide of the war.

His legacy is one of strategic brilliance and quiet determination, earning him recognition as one of the most effective naval commanders of the Pacific War.

Admiral Lord Louis Mountbatten: The Southeast Asia Commander

Admiral Lord Mountbatten, a British aristocrat and skilled military leader, commanded Allied forces in Southeast Asia (SEAC) from 1943. Tasked with recapturing Burma and reopening the Burma Road, he navigated difficult terrain, logistical challenges, and political tensions among British, Indian, and Chinese forces.

Admiral Louis Mountbatten (left) with General of the Army Douglas MacArthur (right)

Known for his charisma and diplomatic skills, Mountbatten built consensus among diverse Allied forces while executing a successful campaign that led to Burma's recapture in 1945. His legacy is one of leadership and diplomacy, playing a crucial role in the Allied victory in Southeast Asia.

◻ **DID YOU KNOW**

- *Mountbatten was a great-grandson of Queen Victoria. His godfather was Tsar Nicholas II.*

- *When visiting Pearl Harbor before the Japanese attack, he was shocked by a perceived lack of security and readiness. This prompted him to think America would be dragged into the war by a surprise attack by Japan. His prediction was dismissed but 3 months later, he was proven to be correct.*

Field Marshal Sir William Slim: The "Forgotten Army" Commander

Field Marshal Slim, commander of the Fourteenth Army in Burma, was a humble and empathetic leader who inspired deep loyalty among his troops. Tasked with recapturing Burma from Japan, he overcame harsh terrain, logistical challenges, and fierce resistance, leading his forces to victory in 1945.

Field Marshal Sir William Slim, General Officer Commanding Fourteenth Army in Burma, 5 March 1945

Known for his "forgotten army" speech, Slim praised the sacrifices of his often-overlooked soldiers. A master of jungle warfare, his legacy is one of resilience, leadership, and strategic brilliance, making him one of Britain's most respected generals of the war.

Chiang Kai-shek: The Leader of Nationalist China

Chiang Kai-shek, leader of China's Nationalist government, was a complex and controversial figure in World War II. While resisting Japan's invasion, he also prioritized fighting Chinese Communists, straining relations with his allies.

Chiang Kai-shek

His leadership was marked by authoritarianism, political maneuvering, and corruption, yet China's resistance tied down large Japanese forces, aiding the broader Pacific War effort. Despite his wartime role, Chiang's legacy remains divisive, culminating in his 1949 defeat in the Chinese Civil War.

◻ **DID YOU KNOW**

- *When Chiang's Nationalist forces were defeated by the Communists, he was forced to retreat to Taiwan in 1949, where he established the Republic of China government, which he ruled until 1975.*

Axis Leaders

Admiral Isoroku Yamamoto: The Architect of Pearl Harbor

Admiral Yamamoto, architect of Pearl Harbor, was a brilliant strategist yet skeptical of war with the U.S., recognizing its superior industrial power. As Commander-in-Chief of the Combined Fleet from 1939, he planned the surprise attack to cripple the U.S. Pacific Fleet and secure Japan's early advantage.

Admiral Isoroku Yamamoto

Known for strategic innovation and calculated risks, Yamamoto opposed the mistreatment of prisoners and cared for his men. His death in 1943, when U.S. forces ambushed his plane, dealt a major blow to Japan's Navy and marked a turning point in the war.

◻ **DID YOU KNOW**

- *Yamamoto studied at Harvard University in the United States and was appointed naval attaché to the Japanese embassy in Washington. He understood that naval power relied on oil and industrial capacity, and that Japan thus had little hope to defeat the U.S. in a war.*

General Hideki Tojo: The Prime Minister

General Tojo, Japan's Prime Minister (1941–1944), led the nation through its most aggressive expansion, spearheading the attack on Pearl Harbor and the war effort. A staunch nationalist and militarist, he was unwavering in his loyalty to the emperor and Japan's imperial ambitions.

Hideki Tojo, Japanese War Crimes Trial

Tojo's authoritarian rule and refusal to compromise isolated Japan, contributing to its eventual defeat and his downfall.

▫ DID YOU KNOW

- *On September 11, 1945 Tojo attempted suicide but despite shooting directly through a charcoal mark on his chest, the bullet missed his heart! He was later tried for war crimes, found guilty and hanged on December 23, 1948.*

General Tadamichi Kuribayashi: The Defender of Iwo Jima

General Tadamichi Kuribayashi, commander of Japanese forces on Iwo Jima (1945), knew the island's defense was a desperate last stand against overwhelming U.S. firepower. A veteran of China, he abandoned traditional banzai charges, instead devising a defensive strategy using tunnels and bunkers to maximize American casualties.

General Tadamichi Kuribayashi

Known for his tactical brilliance and courage, Kuribayashi understood defeat was inevitable but fought to make the U.S. pay dearly. His defense, though unsuccessful, is regarded as a masterpiece of defensive warfare.

◻ **DID YOU KNOW**

- *It is believed that Kuribayashi was killed in action while leading his soldiers in a night-attack on American troops, but his body was never identified. U.S. Marine Corps General Holland Smith said: "Of all our adversaries in the Pacific, Kuribayashi was the most redoubtable."*

- *During the lead up to the attack on Pearl Harbor, Kuribayashi is known to have repeatedly told his family, "America is the last country in the world Japan should fight."*

Admiral Chuichi Nagumo: The Carrier Fleet Commander

Admiral Nagumo, commander of the Japanese carrier fleet at Pearl Harbor, was a skilled but cautious leader. His strict adherence to the attack plan led to a missed opportunity to deal a more decisive blow to the U.S. Pacific Fleet.

At Midway, his indecisiveness and tactical errors contributed to Japan's catastrophic defeat, marking a turning point in the war. His later career was marred by setbacks, and he took his own life during the Battle of Saipan (1944).

General Masaharu Homma: The Conqueror of the Philippines

General Masaharu Homma led the Japanese invasion of the Philippines (1941–1942). A skilled diplomat and strategist, he oversaw Japan's victory but was later held responsible for the Bataan Death March, where thousands of American and Filipino POWs died under brutal conditions. Convicted of war crimes, he was executed by firing squad on April 3, 1946.

▫ DID YOU KNOW

- *Homma spent eight years as a military attaché in the United Kingdom. In 1917, he was attached to the East Lancashire Regiment, and in 1918, served with the British Expeditionary Force in France, being awarded the Military Cross.*

General Tomoyuki Yamashita: The "Tiger of Malaya"

General Yamashita, the "Tiger of Malaya," led Japan's swift conquest of Malaya and Singapore in 1942, using bold tactics and deception. Despite his early success, his later commands in the Philippines and Manchuria were less effective against overwhelming Allied forces. Convicted of war crimes for atrocities like the Manila Massacre, he was hanged on February 23, 1946.

Admiral Takeo Kurita: The Commander at Leyte Gulf

Admiral Kurita was a senior Japanese naval officer who commanded the Center Force during the Battle of Leyte Gulf in October 1944. He played a key role in Operation Sho-Go, Japan's desperate attempt to repel the U.S. invasion of the Philippines.

At the Battle off Samar (part of the action at Leyte Gulf), Kurita's powerful fleet of battleships and cruisers, including the massive Yamato, unexpectedly engaged a much smaller American escort carrier group (Taffy 3). Despite overwhelming firepower, Kurita ultimately withdrew, believing he was facing a much stronger U.S. fleet, missing a chance to crush the vulnerable U.S. invasion force.

CHAPTER 8: THE ATTACK ON PEARL HARBOR – THE WAR BEGINS

The attack on Pearl Harbor on December 7, 1941, is a date etched in infamy in American history. It was a day that shattered the illusion of peace and thrust the United States into the cauldron of World War II. The surprise attack, launched in two waves with a total of 353 aircraft, meticulously planned and executed by the Japanese Imperial Navy Air Service, targeted the heart of the U.S. Pacific Fleet at Pearl Harbor, Hawaii, leaving a trail of devastation and forever altering the course of history.

Aerial view of the U.S. Naval Operating Base, Pearl Harbor, looking southwest on October 30, 1941. Ford Island Naval Air Station is in the center, with the Pearl Harbor Navy Yard just beyond it, across the channel. The airfield in the upper left-center is the U.S. Army's Hickam Field.

Aerial view of the U.S. Naval Operating Base, Pearl Harbor, looking southwest on October 30, 1941. Ford Island Naval Air Station is in the center, with the Pearl

Harbor Navy Yard just beyond it, across the channel. The airfield in the upper left-center is the U.S. Army's Hickam Field.

Japan's Gamble: The Plan to Strike First

The attack on Pearl Harbor was not an act of blind aggression. It was a calculated risk, a bold military strategy designed to cripple the United States before it could enter the war.

Japan's leaders knew they could not win a prolonged conflict against the industrial might of the United States. However, they believed that if they struck hard enough and fast enough, America would be forced to negotiate peace rather than fight a long war.

The plan was the brainchild of Admiral Isoroku Yamamoto, a brilliant strategist who understood the power of America's vast resources. He had studied in the United States and knew that if war dragged on, Japan would be outproduced and outgunned.

To have any chance of success, Japan needed to destroy the U.S. Pacific Fleet in one swift blow, gain control of resource-rich territories in Southeast Asia, and Fortify its defensive perimeter before America could recover.

The attack on Pearl Harbor was the first step in this plan.

The Attack: A Perfectly Executed Ambush

The Journey to Hawaii: Japan's Secret Strategy

To ensure complete surprise, Japan's fleet sailed 4,000 miles across the Pacific in total secrecy. The fleet consisted of:

- 6 aircraft carriers (Akagi, Kaga, Soryu, Hiryu, Shokaku, and Zuikaku).
- 353 aircraft, including bombers, torpedo planes, and fighters.

- Submarines and battleships to support the attack.

To avoid detection, the fleet took a northern route, staying out of shipping lanes. Radio silence was strictly enforced, and Japanese warships communicated only with signal flags.

By December 6, they were in position. The next morning, they launched their first wave of attacks.

The First Wave (7:55 AM): Devastation Begins

The first wave of the attack, launched at 7:55 AM on December 7, 1941, consisted of 183 aircraft, including dive bombers, torpedo planes, and fighters. The aircraft, launched from six aircraft carriers positioned north of Oahu Island, approached Pearl Harbor under the cover of darkness and radio silence.

USS Shaw exploding, Pearl Harbor

The first wave's primary targets were the battleships moored in Battleship Row and the airfields at Hickam Field and Wheeler Field. The dive bombers, armed with armor-piercing bombs, aimed to cripple the battleships, while the torpedo planes, carrying specially modified torpedoes designed for the shallow waters of

Pearl Harbor, targeted their vulnerable hulls. The fighters provided air cover and strafed ground targets, adding to the chaos and confusion.

The first wave's attack was devastatingly effective. Within minutes, the battleships in Battleship Row were engulfed in flames and explosions, as torpedoes and bombs found their marks. Hundreds of aircraft destroyed or damaged on the ground at Hickam and Wheeler.

The results were devastating:

- The USS Oklahoma capsized, trapping more than 400 sailors inside.
- The USS Arizona suffered a direct hit, killing 1,177 men instantly.
- More than 180 U.S. aircraft were destroyed on the ground.

The Second Wave (8:40 AM): Finishing the Job

The second wave of the attack, launched at 8:54 AM, consisted of 170 aircraft, including horizontal bombers, dive bombers, and fighters. The second wave's mission was to reinforce the initial attack, target other military installations, and further cripple the U.S. Pacific Fleet.

A small boat rescues a seaman from the 31,800 ton USS West Virginia burning in the foreground.

The horizontal bombers, carrying high-explosive bombs, targeted the naval shipyard, the submarine base, and the fuel depot. The dive bombers attacked the surviving battleships in Battleship Row, inflicting further damage and casualties. The fighters continued to provide air cover and strafe ground targets.

By 9:45 AM, the attack was over. In just 1 hour and 15 minutes, the U.S. Pacific Fleet had suffered one of the worst military defeats in American history.

The Aftermath: America Awakens

The attack on Pearl Harbor was a stunning tactical success but a strategic disaster for Japan.

American Losses

- 2,403 Americans killed.
- 1,178 wounded.
- 21 U.S. ships damaged or destroyed.

- 188 aircraft destroyed.

The Japanese attack on Pearl Harbor achieved its primary objective of inflicting significant damage on the U.S. Pacific Fleet. Eight battleships were sunk or damaged, including the USS Arizona, which exploded and sank with the loss of over 1,100 lives. Hundreds of aircraft were also destroyed or damaged, and numerous other military installations were targeted.

However, the attack had failed to deliver a knockout blow. The Japanese had focused on battleships, considered the backbone of naval power at the time. They had overlooked the importance of aircraft carriers, which were absent from Pearl Harbor on the day of the attack.

The survival of the aircraft carriers proved to be a crucial factor in the U.S. Navy's ability to recover from the attack and launch counteroffensives against the Japanese. The carriers, with their ability to project air power across vast distances, became the decisive weapon in the naval war in the Pacific, playing a key role in battles like Midway and the Coral Sea.

Japan's Fatal Miscalculation

Japan's bold gamble at Pearl Harbor was based on a flawed assumption - that America would be too demoralized to fight back. Instead, it had the opposite effect. The next day, on December 8, 1941, President Franklin D. Roosevelt, in his address to Congress the day after the attack, declared December 7, 1941, "a date which will live in infamy" and called on Congress to declare war on Japan, shaking off its former isolationism. Congress responded swiftly, formally declaring war on Japan later that same day, and within days, Germany and Italy declared war on the U.S. The Pacific War had begun.

☐ **DID YOU KNOW**

- *Admiral Hara Tadaichi summed up the Japanese result by saying, "We won a great tactical victory at Pearl Harbor and thereby lost the war."*

How the U.S. Underestimated the Threat from Japan

The attack on Pearl Harbor was not entirely unexpected. The United States knew that war with Japan was likely, but it failed to predict when, where, and how the Japanese would strike.

Before December 7, 1941, most U.S. military leaders believed Pearl Harbor was too far away for a Japanese attack, being 4,000 miles away from Japan. U.S. intelligence assumed that if Japan attacked, it would be in the Philippines or Southeast Asia, not Hawaii. Many U.S. military officials dismissed Japan's naval capabilities, believing the Japanese lacked the technology and training to launch a carrier-based surprise attack.

This false sense of security meant that Pearl Harbor's defenses were not at full alert, leaving battleships lined up like sitting ducks in the harbor.

The U.S. had successfully broken Japan's diplomatic code and was intercepting top-secret Japanese messages. However, the "13-part message" sent by Japan to its Washington embassy (which signaled the end of diplomacy) was intercepted, but it was not translated until too late.

American military planners had a deep-seated belief in U.S. naval superiority. They saw Japan as an inferior power, despite its rapid military expansion. U.S. officials assumed Japan would not dare attack a country as powerful as the United States. They failed to recognize Japan's bold, offensive-minded military strategy, which prioritized striking first to gain the upper hand.

This underestimation of Japan's willingness to take risks led to the lack of urgency in preparing for a surprise attack.

Reports of suspicious Japanese activities were ignored or dismissed as unimportant.

For example, a U.S. Navy report on Japanese aircraft carrier movements in late November was not widely distributed to key decision-makers. Warnings from

British intelligence about Japan's aggressive stance in the Pacific were not acted upon quickly enough.

Even on the day of the attack, warnings were ignored! At 3:42 AM, hours before the aerial assault, a U.S. Navy patrol boat spotted a Japanese midget submarine trying to enter Pearl Harbor. The USS Ward, a destroyer, engaged and sank the intruding submarine. The event was reported up the chain of command, but it was not taken seriously enough to trigger a base-wide alert.

Had this warning been treated as a real threat, Pearl Harbor might have been on high alert by the time the air raid began.

❏ **DID YOU KNOW**

- *The Americans fired the first shots at Pearl Harbor. The sinking of the midget submarine made it not only the first shot fired on that day, but the first official American shots in the War.*

The Toll on the Pacific Fleet: A Navy in Ruins

In less than two hours, the United States Pacific Fleet had suffered one of the worst military disasters in American history. The attack, executed with precision and brutality, had crippled the U.S. Navy's ability to respond to Japan's rapid expansion across the Pacific.

The statistics of destruction were staggering:

- 21 ships were damaged or destroyed.
- More than 300 aircraft were destroyed or severely damaged.
- 2,403 Americans were killed, and 1,178 were wounded.

The once-mighty battleship force of the Pacific Fleet was in ruins.

The Battleships: America's Backbone Broken

These massive battleships, symbols of American naval strength, suffered the worst devastation of the Japanese attack.

- **USS Arizona (BB-39): The Greatest Tragedy**

- A 1,760-pound armor-piercing bomb struck the forward magazine, causing a catastrophic explosion.

- The ship broke in half and sank within minutes.

- 1,177 sailors and Marines were killed, nearly half of all casualties that day.

The USS Arizona burning after the Japanese attack. The ship is resting on the harbor bottom.

❏ **DID YOU KNOW**

- *Surviving USS Arizona veterans can choose to have their ashes deposited by divers beneath one of sunken Arizona's gun turrets.*

- *The USS Arizona had 23 sets of brothers serving aboard. There were 37 different families in pairs or trios for a total of 77 men. Only 15 of them survived.*

USS Oklahoma (BB-37): A Watery Tomb

- Hit by multiple torpedoes, the ship capsized within 12 minutes.
- Over 400 sailors were trapped inside as the ship flipped over.
- Rescuers worked for days, cutting through the hull to free survivors, but many died in the darkness.

USS West Virginia (BB-48) and USS California (BB-44): Badly Damaged, But Salvageable

- Both ships were hit by torpedoes and bombs, sinking slowly in the harbor.
- Fires raged on their decks, fed by leaking oil.
- They were later raised, repaired, and returned to battle.

The Other Casualties: Cruisers, Destroyers, and Submarines

While battleships bore the brunt of the attack, other vessels also suffered heavy damage.

- The USS Helena (CL-50) was struck by a torpedo, crippling its hull.
- The USS Utah (BB-31), a former battleship turned target ship, was hit and capsized, killing 58 crew members.
- Several destroyers and smaller vessels were bombed, rendering them inoperable for months.

Although aircraft carriers had miraculously escaped destruction (since they were out at sea), the loss of battleships and support ships left the U.S. Navy severely weakened in the Pacific.

The Airfields: The Sky Lost Before It Could Fight

Japanese pilots targeted Hickam Field, Wheeler Field, and other U.S. air bases, ensuring that American planes could not take off and fight back.

The destruction was complete:

- 188 aircraft destroyed on the ground.
- Many were bombed before pilots could even reach them.
- Some brave American pilots, like Lieutenant Kenneth Taylor and George Welch, managed to take off in their P-40 Warhawks and shoot down Japanese bombers, but they were the exception, not the rule.

With most planes destroyed, the U.S. was left vulnerable to further attacks.

The Shockwaves of Pearl Harbor: A Nation Transformed

Before December 7, 1941, the United States had been deeply divided over the question of war. Many Americans wanted to stay out of the conflict in Europe and Asia - the country had suffered through the Great Depression, and many believed war would only bring more hardship. President Roosevelt had supported Britain and China against the Axis, but he had promised not to send American soldiers into another world war unless directly provoked.

Pearl Harbor changed everything overnight.

A Wave of Patriotism and Outrage

Across the country, Americans were shocked, furious, and ready for action. Recruitment offices overflowed with young men eager to enlist. Factories, which had been producing goods for peacetime, shifted overnight to wartime production. Families hung blue star banners in their windows, signaling that a loved one had gone to fight.

The attack had unified a deeply divided nation in a way nothing else could have.

The Mobilization of the Military

Before the attack, the U.S. had the 17th-largest military in the world - smaller than Portugal's. The U.S. Army had fewer than 200,000 active troops.

By the end of the war, over 16 million Americans would serve in the armed forces.

New military training camps sprang up overnight. The draft expanded, requiring all men aged 18-45 to register. Women enlisted in the military for the first time in large numbers, joining the Women's Army Corps (WACs) and Navy WAVES.

▢ **DID YOU KNOW**

- *Within 30 days of the attack on Pearl Harbor, 134,000 Americans had enlisted in the military!*

The United States was no longer a nation debating war - it was a nation preparing to win it.

CHAPTER 9: EARLY JAPANESE VICTORIES AND ALLIED DEFEATS

The opening months of the Pacific War were a time of triumph for Japan and a period of shocking setbacks for the Allies, particularly the British. Japan's military machine, honed by years of conflict in China and fueled by a potent mix of nationalist fervor and strategic cunning, unleashed a series of lightning-fast offensives that swept across Southeast Asia and the Pacific, capturing key territories and inflicting heavy losses on the unprepared Allied forces.

The Fall of Hong Kong: A Symbolic Loss (December 8–25, 1941)

Just days after the attack on Pearl Harbor, Japanese forces launched a swift and decisive assault on Hong Kong, a British colony since 1841. Defended by a mix of British, Canadian, and Indian troops, Hong Kong was ill-prepared for the Japanese onslaught and fell within weeks, a symbolic loss for the British Empire and a strategic gain for Japan.

The fall of Hong Kong demonstrated Japan's military prowess and its determination to expand its empire at the expense of Western colonial powers. It was a demoralizing blow to the British, who were already struggling to contain the German advance in Europe.

The Japanese Invasion of the Philippines (December 8, 1941 – May 1942)

Japan launched its blitzkrieg across the Pacific in late 1941, with the Philippines one of its primary targets. An American-controlled territory, the Philippines was a strategic stronghold in the Pacific, blocking Japan's route toward Australia and other Allied positions.

On December 8, 1941 - just hours after the attack on Pearl Harbor - Japanese bombers rained destruction on Clark Airfield and other U.S. bases in the Philippines. Within days, Japan launched a full-scale invasion, landing over 100,000 troops on the northern islands and quickly overwhelming Filipino and American defenses.

General Douglas MacArthur, the commanding officer in the Philippines, had hoped to hold off the Japanese forces. However, the speed and force of Japan's assault forced him to retreat to the Bataan Peninsula, where he and his troops would make their stand.

The Battle of Bataan: A Desperate Defense (January – April 1942)

With the fall of Manila on January 2, 1942, American and Filipino forces fell back to Bataan, a jungle-covered peninsula where they planned to fight a prolonged defensive war.

The U.S. and Philippine Army forces on Bataan numbered approximately 76,000 troops. Their defensive positions were naturally fortified by rugged terrain, making direct assaults challenging. Their strategy was to hold out until American reinforcements could arrive.

Japanese flamethrower in action

However, the defenders faced overwhelming odds. General Masaharu Homma's Japanese forces outnumbered and outgunned them, while food and medical supplies dwindled. Starvation and disease took a devastating toll, with thousands succumbing to dysentery, malaria, and exhaustion before even engaging the enemy.

Despite these hardships, American and Filipino troops held out for nearly four months, relying on guerrilla tactics and desperate counterattacks to slow the Japanese advance.

The Fall of Bataan (April 9, 1942)

By April 1942, the defenders of Bataan were on the verge of collapse. Supplies were exhausted, and many soldiers were too weak to continue fighting. General MacArthur had already escaped to Australia, leaving General Edward King in command.

Realizing that further resistance would only lead to unnecessary deaths, King made the difficult decision to surrender.

On April 9, 1942, the largest surrender of U.S. troops in history took place, with over 76,000 American and Filipino soldiers laying down their arms. The Japanese, unprepared to handle such a large number of prisoners, responded with cruelty and indifference. What followed was one of the most infamous war crimes of World War II—the Bataan Death March.

The Bataan Death March: A Journey Through Hell

The captured soldiers expected to be treated according to the rules of war. Instead, they endured one of the most brutal forced marches in military history—the infamous Bataan Death March.

Over 65 miles, American and Filipino POWs were subjected to relentless beatings, starvation, and dehydration as they were marched to a Japanese prison camp.

Thousands perished along the way, reflecting the brutality of the Japanese military and its disregard for the laws of war.

The Bataan Death March became a symbol of Japanese atrocities in the Philippines, strengthening the Allies' resolve to defeat Japan and liberate the islands.

One survivor, Private Lester Tenney, recalled:

"If you fell, you died. If you begged for water, you died. If you tried to help a fellow soldier, you died."

Of the 76,000 prisoners, nearly 10,000 died on the march. Many more perished in the brutal prison camps where they were held.

Prisoner of War Camps: Life After the March

For those who survived the march, the nightmare was not over. Many were sent to hellish POW camps, where they were beaten, tortured, and starved. Some were shipped to Japan to work as slave laborers in mines and factories. Thousands more died from disease, starvation, and mistreatment.

Survivors of these camps would later testify about the horrors they endured, leading to war crimes trials after the war.

America's Response: A Vow for Revenge

The fall of the Philippines was a humiliating blow to the United States. However, the brutality of the Bataan Death March ignited a fierce determination to fight back.

Before leaving the Philippines, General MacArthur made a solemn vow:

"I shall return."

These words became a rallying cry for American forces. The liberation of the Philippines became a top priority for U.S. military planners.

The Malayan Campaign: A Blitzkrieg in the Jungle (December 8, 1941 – February 15, 1942)

The Japanese invasion of Malaya (present-day Malaysia) in December 1941 was a textbook example of a blitzkrieg, a lightning-fast offensive that exploited speed, surprise, and maneuverability to overwhelm the enemy. The Japanese forces, employing a combination of tanks, bicycles, and infantry, rapidly advanced down the Malay Peninsula, outmaneuvering and outgunning the British defenders.

The British, caught off guard and unprepared for the Japanese tactics, suffered a series of defeats, culminating in the fall of Singapore in February 1942. The loss of Singapore, a strategic fortress and symbol of British power in Asia, was a humiliating blow to the British Empire and a major propaganda victory for Japan.

The Battle for Singapore (February 1942): The Final Stand

By January 31, 1942, British forces had completely retreated to Singapore - their last hope of resistance in Southeast Asia.

With 85,000 British, Indian, and Australian troops, and defenses including massive coastal guns and fortified positions, British commanders believed Singapore could hold out indefinitely. Singapore's. The island had never fallen to an enemy before.

However, there was a fatal flaw - Singapore's defenses were built to repel a naval attack from the south, while the Japanese attacked from the north, across the Johor Strait.

The Japanese Assault Begins (February 8, 1942)

On the night of February 8, 1942, Japan launched its final assault. Thousands of Japanese troops crossed the Johor Strait in small boats, overwhelming British defensive positions. British forces, exhausted and demoralized, were unable to stop the rapid Japanese advance. Singapore's water supply was bombed, leaving defenders with no fresh drinking water.

By February 13, the British had been pushed back to the city center. The once-glorious colony was now a battlefield of fire, rubble, and corpses.

The Surrender: Britain's Greatest Defeat (February 15, 1942)

On February 15, 1942, British General Arthur Percival faced an unthinkable decision. His troops were exhausted, starving, and out of ammunition. Singapore's civilians were dying by the thousands from bombing and starvation. The Japanese had cut off all escape routes.

At 5:15 PM, Percival walked into the Ford Motor Factory, where General Yamashita waited.

He surrendered Singapore to Japan, marking Britain's worst military defeat in history.

Lieutenant-General Percival (2nd right) and his party carry the Union flag on their way to surrender Singapore to the Japanese

The Aftermath: A City in Chains

80,000 British, Indian, and Australian troops became prisoners of war - the largest British surrender in history. Singapore was renamed "Syonan-to" (Light of the South), and its people were subjected to years of Japanese occupation and terror.

Tens of thousands of Singaporean Chinese civilians were rounded up and executed in the Sook Ching massacre. This was a systematic purge of 'anti-Japanese' elements.

Many POWs were sent to the Thai-Burma Railway, undertaking brutal slave labor, where thousands died of starvation, disease, and torture.

Women and children also suffered under Japanese rule, with many subjected to brutal violence.

Singapore, once the crown jewel of the British Empire in Asia, had become a city of suffering.

Wake Island (December 8 – 23, 1941)

The Battle of Wake Island, a small atoll in the vast expanse of the Pacific Ocean, was a microcosm of the early stages of World War II. It was a story of David versus Goliath, of a small but determined garrison of U.S. Marines and civilian contractors facing a relentless onslaught from a powerful Japanese invasion force. The battle, though ultimately ending in a Japanese victory, showed the courage and resilience of the American defenders, who fought against overwhelming odds and inflicted significant losses on the enemy.

Wake Island was an American territory located about 2,300 miles west of Hawaii and 1,500 miles east of Guam. Despite its small size and remote location, Wake Island held strategic importance for the United States in the Pacific.

The island served as a refueling stop for Pan American Airways' transpacific flights, a vital link in the communication and transportation network between the United States and Asia. It also housed a small military garrison, consisting of U.S.

Marines, sailors, and civilian contractors, who were responsible for maintaining the airfield and other facilities on the island.

For Japan, capturing Wake Island was crucial for several reasons. It would eliminate a potential threat to its eastern flank, as the island could be used as a base for American air and naval operations against Japanese forces in the Marshall Islands and the Gilbert Islands. It would secure a valuable refueling and supply depot for Japanese forces operating in the central Pacific. It would also serve as a propaganda victory, demonstrating Japan's military prowess and its ability to strike at American territories.

The Japanese Invasion: A Determined Assault

The Japanese attack began on December 8, 1941, just hours after the attack on Pearl Harbor. The invasion force, commanded by Rear Admiral Sadamichi Kajioka, consisted of three light cruisers, six destroyers, two patrol boats, and two transports carrying over 450 Special Naval Landing Force troops.

The initial Japanese attack was met with fierce resistance from the American defenders, who were outnumbered but determined to hold their ground. The Marines, armed with six 5-inch coastal defense guns and twelve 3-inch anti-aircraft guns, inflicted significant damage on the Japanese ships, forcing them to withdraw.

However, the Japanese were not deterred. They returned the next day with reinforcements, including aircraft carriers, and launched a second attack. The American defenders, now facing air strikes as well as naval bombardment, continued to fight back, but their situation was becoming increasingly desperate.

The Marines, led by Major James P. S. Devereux, inflicted heavy casualties on the Japanese landing force, using their limited resources and their knowledge of the terrain to their advantage.

The civilian contractors also played a crucial role in the defense of Wake Island. They repaired damaged equipment, constructed fortifications, and even manned anti-aircraft guns, contributing to the island's resistance.

However, the defenders' position was ultimately untenable. The Japanese, with their superior firepower and relentless attacks, gradually wore down the defenders' resistance. On December 23, 1941, after two weeks of fierce fighting, Major Devereux surrendered Wake Island to the Japanese.

▢ *DID YOU KNOW*

- *Fewer than 100 Americans died in the Battle of Wake Island, while the Japanese lost between 900 and 1,000.*

Thailand and Indochina (December 1941)

While the world's attention was focused on the dramatic events unfolding in the Pacific in late 1941 and early 1942, Japan was also making significant strategic moves in mainland Southeast Asia. The occupation of French Indochina and the alliance with Thailand were crucial steps in Japan's southward expansion, securing vital resources and strategic advantages for its war effort.

French Indochina, comprising modern-day Vietnam, Laos, and Cambodia, a French colony, was rich in natural resources, including rubber, rice, and minerals. It was a valuable asset for France, but it also held strategic importance for Japan's expansionist ambitions.

Japan had been gradually increasing its influence in Indochina since the 1930s, exploiting France's weakness during World War II to secure concessions and establish a military presence in the colony. In September 1940, Japan pressured the Vichy French government, which collaborated with Nazi Germany, to allow Japanese troops to enter and establish bases in northern Indochina.

In July 1941, Japan completed its occupation of French Indochina, seizing control of the entire colony and securing access to its valuable resources and strategic locations.

The occupation of Indochina was a significant step in Japan's southward expansion, providing a staging ground for its subsequent invasions of Malaya, Singapore, and the Dutch East Indies.

On December 8, 1941, just hours after the attack on Pearl Harbor, Japan invaded Thailand. The Thai government, after a brief resistance, signed an armistice with Japan and allowed Japanese troops to pass through its territory to invade Malaya and Burma.

Guam (December 8 – 10, 1941)

The capture of Guam in December 1941 was a swift and strategic victory for Japan in the opening days of the Pacific War. The small island, an American territory since 1898, held a significant position in the western Pacific, and its fall to the Japanese not only provided a valuable base for their expanding empire but also dealt a symbolic blow to American power in the region. The battle for Guam, though brief, highlighted the effectiveness of Japan's early war strategy and the challenges faced by the U.S. in defending its far-flung territories.

The invasion force of around 5,900 troops from the South Seas Detachment, launched a two-pronged assault on the island. The American defenders, outnumbered and outgunned, put up a valiant resistance, but their efforts were hampered by the lack of adequate defenses and the swiftness of the Japanese advance.

The Japanese forces quickly overwhelmed the American defenders, capturing key positions and pushing inland. The fighting was intense but brief, with the outnumbered Marines and sailors unable to hold back the Japanese onslaught.

On December 10, 1941, just two days after the initial attack, the American commander, Captain George McMillin, surrendered Guam to the Japanese.

Rabaul (January 23, 1942)

The capture of Rabaul in January 1942 solidified Japan's control over the vital territory of New Britain and establishing a formidable base for further expansion in the Southwest Pacific. The fall of Rabaul, a key Allied outpost, exposed the vulnerability of Australia and its neighboring territories.

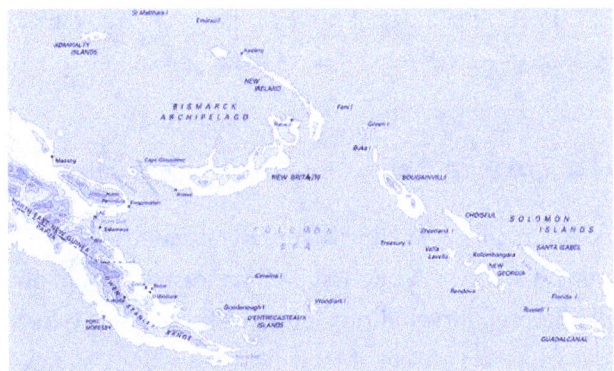
Rabaul, located on the island of New Britain in the Bismarck Archipelago

Rabaul, located on the island of New Britain in the Bismarck Archipelago, was a strategically vital port town with a deep-water harbor and access to crucial sea lanes. The town, under Australian control since World War I, served as a key Allied outpost in the region, housing a naval base, an airfield, and a small garrison of Australian troops.

For Japan, capturing Rabaul was a key objective in its southward expansion strategy. The town's strategic location, its harbor facilities, and its airfield made it an ideal base for supporting operations in the South Pacific, disrupting Allied communication lines, and potentially launching attacks on Australia and New Zealand.

The Japanese invasion of Rabaul began on January 23, 1942, with a force of around 1,400 troops from the South Seas Detachment, supported by a powerful naval and air contingent. The Australian defenders, outnumbered and outgunned, put up a valiant resistance, but their efforts were hampered by the lack of adequate defenses and the swiftness of the Japanese advance.

The Japanese forces quickly captured key positions and pushed inland. The fighting was intense but brief, with the outnumbered Australians unable to hold back the Japanese onslaught.

On January 23, 1942, after a day of fierce fighting, the Australian commander, Colonel John Scanlan, surrendered Rabaul to the Japanese.

The Burma Campaign: A Retreat into the Jungle (January–May 1942)

For Japan, capturing Burma was crucial for several reasons. First, it would secure its eastern flank, protecting its conquests in Southeast Asia from potential Allied counterattacks. Second, it would provide access to Burma's valuable resources, particularly oil, which was essential for Japan's war effort. Third, it would cut off the Burma Road, a vital supply route that the Allies used to transport aid to China's Nationalist government, which was fighting against Japanese aggression.

For the Allies, defending Burma was equally important. The loss of Burma would not only threaten India's eastern border but also jeopardize the flow of supplies to China, weakening its resistance against Japan. The British government, recognizing the strategic significance of Burma, deployed a substantial force of British, Indian, and Commonwealth troops to defend the colony.

The Invasion of Burma (January – May 1942)

The Japanese offensive into Burma was led by General Shojiro Iida, who quickly overwhelmed British and Indian forces.

Japanese troops used swift jungle warfare tactics, bypassing strongholds and attacking weak points. The British were unprepared for Japan's speed and aggression, often retreating before battles could even begin. By March 1942, Japanese forces had captured Rangoon, the capital of Burma, cutting off the Burma Road.

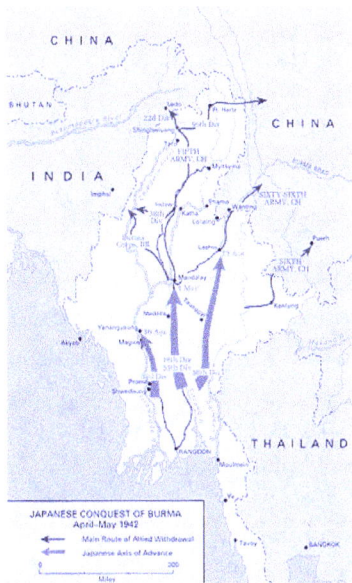

Map of the Japanese Invasion of Burma

The Longest Retreat: British and Chinese Forces in Desperate Flight

With Burma collapsing, British and Chinese forces were forced into a chaotic and demoralizing retreat, over 1,200 miles through dense jungle, mountains, and rivers. It was one of the longest retreats in military history. Thousands of soldiers and civilians died from disease, starvation, and exhaustion. Those who fell behind were captured or executed by Japanese forces.

By May 1942, Burma had completely fallen to Japan.

The Atrocities in Burma

The Japanese encouraged ethnic divisions, pitting Burmese nationalists against British-loyal ethnic groups. Thousands of Indian, Burmese, and British troops were captured and sent to death camps. The construction of the Thai-Burma Railway (the "Death Railway") led to tens of thousands of deaths.

The Japanese Invasion of the Dutch East Indies (January – March 1942)

The Dutch East Indies (modern-day Indonesia) was one of the most resource-rich regions in the world, and for Japan, it was the ultimate prize.

The Dutch East Indies provided not just oil, but rubber, tin, and other crucial war materials. Controlling the islands would allow Japan to cut off Allied supply lines and fortify its defensive perimeter. The islands were also a stepping stone toward further expansion into Australia and the Indian Ocean.

By the time Japan launched its full-scale invasion in early 1942, the Dutch colonial forces stood little chance of holding out.

The Japanese strategy was brutal and efficient.

The Japanese navy overwhelmed Dutch and Allied ships, sinking most of the defending fleet. Japanese forces landed on multiple islands simultaneously, preventing the Dutch from concentrating their defenses. The Japanese bombed key cities, striking fear into the hearts of the defenders.

On January 11, 1942, the first Japanese forces landed in Borneo, quickly capturing the oil-rich city of Tarakan. From there, they swept through the islands with little resistance.

The Battle of the Java Sea: A Decisive Defeat

The Allies attempted to stop Japan's advance in a massive naval engagement - the Battle of the Java Sea on February 27, 1942.

A combined American, British, Dutch, and Australian fleet confronted the Japanese navy, but outnumbered and outgunned, the Allies suffered a crushing defeat. The Dutch flagship De Ruyter was sunk, along with multiple Allied ships.

With naval resistance crushed, the Japanese launched a full-scale invasion of Java, the heart of the Dutch colony.

The Fall of Batavia and the End of Dutch Rule

By March 9, 1942, the Dutch forces, led by Governor-General Tjarda van Starkenborgh Stachouwer, surrendered unconditionally.

Over 100,000 Dutch, British, and Indonesian troops became prisoners of war. Japan took control of the entire Indonesian archipelago, securing its precious oil supplies. Dutch civilians and prisoners of war suffered brutal treatment, with many forced into slave labor.

The conquest of the Dutch East Indies marked one of Japan's greatest military victories, but it would also become one of its greatest liabilities, as resistance movements and guerrilla warfare bled the Japanese occupation forces for years.

A Time of Triumph for Japan

This was a time of triumph for Japan and of shocking setbacks for the Allies, particularly the British. Japan's military prowess, combined with Allied unpreparedness and strategic miscalculations, led to a series of swift and decisive Japanese victories that reshaped the balance of power in Asia and the Pacific.

The brutality of the fighting, the heavy casualties on both sides, and the suffering of civilian populations in occupied territories was a grim reminder of the devastating consequences of war.

The Japanese victories also had a galvanizing effect on the Allies, particularly the United States, which mobilized its vast industrial and military might to turn the tide of the war in its favor. The Pacific War was far from over, but the stage was set for a long and bloody conflict that would ultimately determine the fate of nations and the future of the region.

CHAPTER 10: THE FIRST TURNING POINT – THE BATTLE OF THE CORAL SEA (MAY 4 – 8 1942)

The Battle of the Coral Sea, fought in May 1942, was a pivotal moment in the early stages of the Pacific War, stopping Japan's southward expansion and setting the stage for the crucial Allied victory at Midway a month later.

▫ ***DID YOU KNOW***

- *The Battle of the Coral Sea was the first major naval battle in history fought entirely by aircraft carriers, with opposing ships never sighting each other directly.*

Japan set its sights on Australia. The Imperial Japanese Navy planned to capture Port Moresby in Papua New Guinea, to provide a potential launching point for attacks on northern Australia. This would disrupt Allied supply lines, threaten Australia's security, and potentially force it to divert resources from the war effort in other theaters.

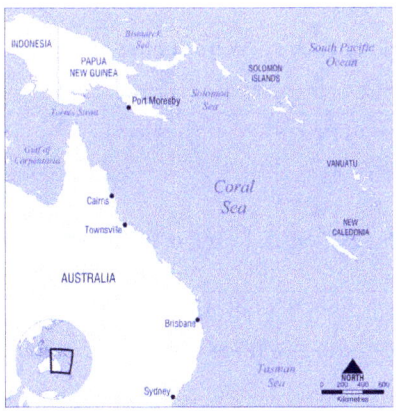

The Coral Sea

Capturing Port Moresby would also give Japan control over the Coral Sea, a strategically important body of water that connected the South Pacific to the Indian Ocean. This would allow Japan to further isolate Australia, disrupt Allied shipping, and strengthen its defensive perimeter.

The U.S. Navy: A Fleet Rebuilding

The U.S. Navy, still reeling from the devastating attack on Pearl Harbor just five months earlier, entered the Battle of the Coral Sea with a sense of urgency and determination. The losses at Pearl Harbor had significantly weakened the Pacific Fleet, but the U.S. Navy's industrial might and its ability to quickly mobilize its resources allowed it to deploy a formidable force to the Coral Sea.

The U.S. Navy's task force, designated Task Force 17, was commanded by Rear Admiral Frank Jack Fletcher and centered around two aircraft carriers:

- **USS Lexington**: A veteran of the early Pacific War, the Lexington was a powerful and well-equipped carrier, carrying over 90 aircraft, including fighters, dive bombers, and torpedo bombers.
- **USS Yorktown**: A newer and slightly smaller carrier than the Lexington, the Yorktown carried over 70 aircraft.

In addition to the carriers, Task Force 17 included a number of cruisers, destroyers, and other support vessels, providing a protective screen for the carriers and contributing to the overall firepower of the fleet.

The Imperial Japanese Navy: A Force on the Offensive

The Imperial Japanese Navy (IJN), flushed with its early successes in the Pacific War, entered the Battle of the Coral Sea with confidence and a sense of invincibility. The IJN's carrier force, a key element of its offensive strategy, was considered to be the most powerful in the world at the time.

The Japanese invasion force, designated the Port Moresby Invasion Force, was commanded by Vice Admiral Shigeyoshi Inoue and included two main carrier divisions:

- **The Fifth Carrier Division:** Commanded by Rear Admiral Takeo Takagi, this division included the fleet carriers Shokaku and Zuikaku, each carrying over 70 aircraft, including fighters, dive bombers, and torpedo bombers.

- **The Shoho Carrier Division:** This division included the light carrier Shoho, which carried a smaller complement of aircraft compared to the fleet carriers.

In addition to the carriers, the Japanese invasion force included a number of cruisers, destroyers, and transports carrying troops and supplies for the planned invasion of Port Moresby.

The Rise of Carrier Warfare

The Battle of the Coral Sea was a landmark encounter not only because it was the first major carrier-versus-carrier battle but also because it showed the growing importance of technological advancements in naval warfare.

Aircraft carriers, with their ability to project air power over long distances, had become the decisive weapon in naval combat, replacing the traditional dominance of battleships. The battle demonstrated the effectiveness of carrier-based aircraft in attacking enemy ships and disrupting their operations.

Both the U.S. Navy and the IJN had invested heavily in developing their carrier aviation capabilities, and the battle showed the latest advancements in aircraft technology, including dive bombers, torpedo bombers, and fighter planes. It also highlighted the importance of radar, a new technology that allowed ships to detect enemy aircraft and vessels at long distances.

The Human Element: Courage and Sacrifice

The battle was not just a clash of machines and technology; it was also a human drama, a story of courage, sacrifice, and loss on both sides of the conflict.

The pilots who flew the attack and defense missions faced tremendous risks, braving enemy fire and the dangers of flying over open water, with many not returning from their missions.

The sailors who manned the ships also faced danger and hardship, enduring long hours, cramped quarters, and the constant threat of attack. They witnessed the destruction of their ships and the loss of their comrades, and they displayed remarkable courage and resilience in the face of adversity.

Initial Actions: Setting the Stage

The Battle of the Coral Sea began with a series of preliminary actions that set the stage for the main carrier engagement. These actions involved reconnaissance missions, air strikes on smaller targets, and the maneuvering of fleets to gain a strategic advantage.

- **Japanese Capture of Tulagi (May 3-4):** The Japanese, aiming to establish a seaplane base in the Solomon Islands, landed troops on the small island of Tulagi, capturing it after a brief resistance from a small Australian garrison. This move provided the Japanese with a forward base for their operations in the Coral Sea, but it also alerted the Allies to their intentions.

- **U.S. Carrier Strikes on Tulagi (May 4):** The U.S. Navy, having detected the Japanese landings on Tulagi, launched air strikes from the carrier USS Yorktown against the Japanese forces on the island. The air strikes sank several Japanese ships and damaged Japanese operations, but they also revealed the presence of the American carriers to the Japanese.

- **The Search for the Enemy Fleets (May 5-6):** Both the U.S. and Japanese fleets, aware of each other's presence in the Coral Sea, began searching for the enemy carriers, using reconnaissance aircraft and scouting vessels. The vast expanse of the Coral Sea and the limited visibility due to weather conditions made the search a challenging and tense affair.

Carrier Engagement: A Clash of Air Power

The main carrier engagement took place on May 7 and 8, 1942. It was a clash of air power, with both sides launching waves of aircraft to attack the enemy carriers and their supporting ships.

- **The Sinking of the Shoho (May 7):** The U.S. Navy, having located the Japanese light carrier Shoho, launched a devastating airstrike from the carriers Lexington and Yorktown. The air strike, consisting of dive bombers and torpedo planes, overwhelmed the Shoho's defenses, sinking the carrier and inflicting heavy losses on its aircraft and crew. This victory, the first sinking of a Japanese carrier in the war, was a significant morale booster for the Allies.

- **The Lexington and Yorktown Damaged (May 8):** The Japanese, retaliating for the loss of the Shoho, launched its own air strikes against the American carriers. The attacks, though hampered by poor weather and communication problems, inflicted significant damage on the Lexington and the Yorktown. The Lexington, crippled by a series of explosions and fires, was ultimately scuttled by the U.S. Navy to prevent it from falling into enemy hands. The Yorktown, though damaged, was able to withdraw and would play a crucial role in the upcoming Battle of Midway.

- **The Shokaku Damaged and the Zuikaku Depleted (May 8):** The U.S. Navy also launched air strikes against the Japanese carriers Shokaku and Zuikaku. The Shokaku was severely damaged and forced to withdraw, while the Zuikaku, though not directly hit, lost a significant number of its aircraft and experienced pilots. These losses would have a significant impact on Japan's ability to participate in the Battle of Midway.

A mushroom cloud rises after a heavy explosion on board the USS Lexington, May 8, 1942.

The Aftermath: A Strategic Turning Point

While tactically inconclusive, the Battle of the Coral Sea was a strategic victory for the Allies. The Japanese, having lost the light carrier Shoho and with significant damage to the Shokaku, were forced to abandon their plan to capture Port Moresby. This prevented them from further isolating Australia and disrupting Allied operations in the South Pacific.

The battle also had a significant impact on the balance of power in the Pacific. The losses suffered by the Japanese at Coral Sea, particularly the damage to the Shokaku and the loss of experienced pilots, significantly weakened their carrier force and contributed to their decisive defeat at Midway just a month later.

The Battle of the Coral Sea was a turning point in the Pacific War, marking the first time that a Japanese offensive had been halted. It demonstrated the growing strength of the U.S. Navy and its ability to challenge Japan's dominance in the Pacific.

CHAPTER 11: THE BATTLE OF MIDWAY (JUNE 4 – 7, 1942)

The Battle of Midway was a pivotal naval battle in the Pacific Theater of World War II. It marked a turning point in the war, as the United States decisively defeated Japan, significantly weakening the IJN. It marked the end of Japan's offensive momentum and the beginning of the Allied counteroffensive.

The Japanese operation for Midway, codenamed Operation MI, had two primary objectives:

- Eliminate the U.S. Pacific Fleet: The attack on Pearl Harbor, while successful in damaging the U.S. fleet, had failed to destroy its aircraft carriers, which were absent from the harbor during the attack. The Japanese saw Midway as an opportunity to lure the remaining American carriers into a decisive battle and eliminate them, securing naval dominance in the Pacific.

- Capture Midway Atoll: Midway Atoll, a strategically located island chain about 1,300 miles northwest of Hawaii, was seen as a valuable prize for Japan. Its capture would extend Japan's defensive perimeter, and operate as a forward base from which Japan could launch air raids on Hawaii, further weakening American defenses. Some Japanese leaders even believed that controlling Midway could force the U.S. into peace negotiations before a full-scale counteroffensive could begin.

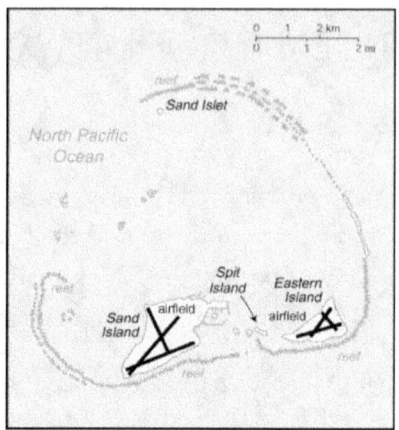

Midway Islands

The Intelligence Breakthrough: How the U.S. Knew Japan's Plans

One of the key reasons for America's success at Midway was intelligence gathering.

The U.S. had cracked Japan's secret naval code (JN-25), allowing American cryptanalysts to intercept and decipher Japanese messages. By late May 1942, Admiral Chester Nimitz, commander of the U.S. Pacific Fleet, had intelligence indicating that Japan was planning an attack on a target referred to as "AF."

To confirm that "AF" referred to Midway, U.S. forces at the atoll sent out a false message claiming their water filtration system had failed. A few days later, Japanese radio transmissions reported that "AF was short on fresh water," confirming Midway as the target. The trap was set.

Armed with this intelligence, Nimitz prepared an ambush.

The U.S. positioned three aircraft carriers - USS Enterprise, USS Hornet, and USS Yorktown - just northeast of Midway. The Japanese, believing the American carriers were still at Pearl Harbor, walked into the trap completely unaware.

The Battle Begins: June 3–4, 1942

On June 3, American long-range bombers launched pre-emptive strikes against the approaching Japanese fleet, but they failed to inflict significant damage.

At dawn on June 4, the Japanese launched 108 aircraft to attack Midway Atoll. The bombing was intense, destroying fuel depots, airstrips, and American defensive positions. However, Midway's anti-aircraft gunners fought back fiercely, preventing total destruction. The Japanese air commander radioed back: "Another strike is needed to finish the job."

This decision would cost Japan dearly.

The initial Japanese attack also revealed their position to the American fleet, which was waiting in ambush nearby. The American carriers, having been alerted by radar and reconnaissance aircraft, launched their own air strikes against the Japanese fleet.

The Turning Point: America's Carrier Strikes (June 4, 1942, Morning)

The American counterattacks, launched from its aircraft carriers, caught the Japanese carriers at a vulnerable moment. The Japanese carriers were in the process of refueling and rearming their aircraft after the attack on Midway, and their decks were crowded with planes and fuel hoses.

The American dive bombers, arriving in waves, targeted the Japanese carriers, scoring direct hits with their bombs. The Akagi, Kaga, and Soryu were all hit and set ablaze, their decks engulfed in flames and explosions.

▫ **DID YOU KNOW**

- *All three U.S. carriers and some supporting vessels benefited from radar, allowing them to detect approaching Japanese aircraft at long range and better prepare for their attacks. In contrast, the Japanese ships relied solely on human lookouts, allowing U.S. dive-bombers to remain undetected until virtually the moment they reached attack position.*

The Final Blow: The Sinking of Hiryū (June 4–5, 1942)

The fourth Japanese carrier, Hiryū, launched two counterstrikes targeting USS Yorktown. Three bombs hit Yorktown in the first attack, causing damage but not disabling the ship. The subsequent second attack forced the crew to abandon ship. (A Japanese submarine later sank the Yorktown on June 7). However, by the afternoon of June 5, American aircraft located and destroyed Hiryū as well, sealing Japan's fate.

USS Yorktown, during the Battle of Midway, June 4, 1942, shortly after she was hit by Japanese bombs, causing the sinking of the aircraft carrier on June 7, 1942, in which 141 men were killed.

By the end of the battle, all four Japanese carriers were sunk with over 300 Japanese aircraft lost. Japan's best carrier pilots - highly trained veterans - were dead.

This crippling loss meant Japan could no longer launch major offensive operations in the Pacific – a setback from which it never recovered.

☐ **DID YOU KNOW**

- U.S. Navy patrols recovered nearly three dozen Japanese crewmen from the *engineering department of the Hiryu. Interrogation of these prisoners of war provided the Americans with vital intelligence about Japanese naval capabilities.*

The Human Cost: Death and Survival

307 American sailors and pilots died. Many of the torpedo bomber crews were lost, sacrificing themselves to ensure the success of the dive bombers.

The Japanese lost more than 3,000 sailors.

Why Midway Changed the War

The Battle of Midway was more than just a naval battle - it was the moment the tide of World War II turned against Japan.

The Japanese defeat at Midway marked the end of their offensive momentum in the Pacific and the beginning of the Allied counteroffensive. The crippling of Japan's naval power allowed the Allies to seize the initiative, launching a series of campaigns that gradually pushed back Japanese forces - from this moment on, Japan was fighting a losing war.

The battle had been won not just through strength, but through intelligence, bravery, and sacrifice.

The road to victory in the Pacific was still long, but Midway made that victory possible.

CHAPTER 12: THE ISLAND HOPPING CAMPAIGN – THE LONG ROAD TO VICTORY

The vast Pacific Ocean, dotted with countless islands, presented a unique challenge for the Allied forces. Instead of engaging in a costly and time-consuming battle for every Japanese-held island, a new strategy emerged: island-hopping. This innovative approach, also known as leap frogging, involved selectively capturing key islands while bypassing others, allowing the Allies to advance across the Pacific and bring the war closer to Japan's doorstep.

The Allies would selectively target key islands, capturing them and transforming them into airfields and naval bases to support further advances toward Japan.

This strategy allowed the Allies to bypass heavily fortified Japanese positions, conserving their resources and minimizing casualties. It also enabled them to disrupt Japanese supply lines, isolate their forces, and gradually tighten the noose around Japan's home islands.

The island-hopping campaign in the Pacific was a complex and arduous undertaking, involving a series of amphibious assaults on strategically important islands held by the Japanese. Each island presented unique challenges, from heavily fortified defenses and treacherous terrain to the fanatical resistance of the Japanese defenders.

Let's take a look at some of the key battles in the Island-Hopping Campaign.

The Battle of Guadalcanal (August 7, 1942 – February 9, 1943)

Guadalcanal was a small, jungle-covered island in the Solomon Islands, north-east of Australia. Seemingly insignificant, in reality, it was a key strategic point.

Guadalcanal was the location of an important airfield, which the Japanese had begun building. If completed, it would allow them to launch attacks on U.S.

supply routes to Australia. If the U.S. captured the island, they could turn it into a base to launch counterattacks against Japan.

Guadalcanal was the first major U.S. offensive in the Pacific, taking the fight to Japan. A victory here would stop Japan's advance and shift momentum to the Allies.

But no one expected just how brutal the battle would be.

Marines rest in the field on Guadalcanal

The Invasion: August 7, 1942 – The U.S. Lands

Before dawn on August 7, 1942, U.S. Marines of the 1st Marine Division climbed into their landing craft, hearts pounding as they prepared to storm Guadalcanal's beaches.

The invasion fleet carried 19,000 Marines, supported by U.S. Navy warships. Expecting heavy resistance, the Marines braced for a bloodbath on the beaches, but to their surprise, they landed with little opposition - the Japanese defenders had retreated into the jungle.

Within two days, the Marines captured the nearly completed airstrip, renaming it Henderson Field after a fallen pilot from the Battle of Midway.

For a moment, it seemed like the battle might be easy.

They were wrong!

Japan Strikes Back: The Bloody Struggle for Henderson Field

The Japanese had no intention of giving up Guadalcanal. Within days, Japanese bombers and warships attacked U.S. positions. Reinforcements arrived by sea, bringing thousands of Japanese soldiers determined to retake the island. For the next six months, Guadalcanal became a nightmare of brutal jungle combat, starvation, and unrelenting warfare.

The Battle of the Tenaru River (August 21, 1942)

The first major Japanese counterattack came at Tenaru River, just east of Henderson Field. At midnight, over 900 Japanese soldiers launched a full-scale Banzai charge, attempting to overrun the Marines. The Americans held their ground, mowing down wave after wave of attackers. By morning, hundreds of Japanese bodies littered the battlefield, marking one of the first clear U.S. victories in the Pacific War.

But this was only the beginning.

The Naval Battle of Savo Island (August 8-9, 1942) – A U.S. Disaster

While the Marines fought on land, a disaster unfolded at sea. Japanese warships launched a surprise night attack, sinking four Allied cruisers and killing over 1,000 sailors. The U.S. Navy was forced to withdraw, leaving the Marines on Guadalcanal without naval support for weeks.

For the Marines, this meant no reinforcements, no fresh supplies, and no easy way off the island.

They were on their own.

▫ **DID YOU KNOW**

- *The waters around Guadalcanal became the site of some of the most intense naval battles of WWII, earning the channel the nickname "Ironbottom Sound" due to the 111 sunken ships! There are also 1,450 downed airplanes.*

The War of Attrition: Hunger, Disease, and Desperation

Life on Guadalcanal was a living nightmare. The jungle proved to be an enemy just as much as the Japanese. Thick, humid air made breathing difficult. Malaria-carrying mosquitoes infected thousands, weakening men before they even faced combat. Mud, rain, and rotting vegetation turned the battlefield into a disease-ridden swamp.

Both sides struggled to get supplies. The Japanese called Guadalcanal "Starvation Island" - thousands of their troops died from hunger before ever firing a shot. Marines survived on spoiled rations and rainwater, fighting off dysentery and exhaustion as much as the enemy.

The Turning Point: The Naval Battles of Guadalcanal (November 12-15, 1942)

By November, Japan made one final attempt to retake Guadalcanal. They launched a massive naval attack, hoping to land 7,000 fresh troops on the island. The U.S. Navy intercepted them, leading to a series of brutal sea battles. Despite heavy U.S. losses, the Japanese reinforcements never reached Guadalcanal.

▫ **DID YOU KNOW**

- *In one battle, the USS Juneau was sunk, killing all five Sullivan brothers. U.S. military policy was later changed to protect surviving family members from combat duty if they had already lost close relatives in military service. The Sullivan's deaths influenced the film Saving Private Ryan.*

The Sullivan brothers on USS Juneau
- Joseph, Francis, Albert, Madison
and George Sullivan

The Final Push: The End of the Battle (February 1943)

With no reinforcements and starvation setting in, Japan finally abandoned Guadalcanal in February 1943. Rather than a final stand, Japan secretly withdrew 10,000 troops in February 1943, admitting defeat but avoiding total destruction.

The battle had cost over 7,000 American lives, and more than 25,000 Japanese dead, many from starvation and disease. Dozens of U.S. and Japanese warships sunk in brutal naval combat.

But it was a decisive victory for the Allies. Japan's unstoppable advance had been broken, and the U.S. gained its first major foothold in the Pacific.

Guadalcanal was the first step in winning back the Pacific.

The Cost of Victory

For those who survived Guadalcanal, the war never truly left them. Many suffered from PTSD, haunted by the horrors of jungle combat. Some never recovered from the starvation, disease, and exhaustion they endured on the island. For the

Japanese, Guadalcanal was a brutal lesson in defeat - one that would lead to even more desperate resistance in battles to come.

Guadalcanal wasn't just a battle—it was a test of will, endurance, and survival. For six months, it was a nightmare of jungle warfare, naval battles, disease, and death.

And for those who fought there, it was a memory that would never fade.

Battle of Tarawa (November 20–23, 1943): The First Test of Island Hopping

The Battle of Tarawa stands out as a particularly bloody and significant engagement. This small atoll in the Gilbert Islands became a testing ground for the island-hopping strategy, a microcosm of courage, resilience, and the devastating cost of the war in the Pacific.

Tarawa Atoll, a collection of small islands in the central Pacific, held strategic significance for both the Allies and Japan. For the Allies, capturing Tarawa would provide a valuable airfield and staging point for further operations in the Marshall Islands, bringing them closer to the Japanese mainland. For Japan, Tarawa was a key link in its outer defensive perimeter, protecting its access to vital resources in Southeast Asia and its communication lines with its forces in the South Pacific.

The Battle of Tarawa began on November 20, 1943, with a massive amphibious assault by U.S. Marines. The Marines, supported by naval bombardment and air strikes, faced a formidable challenge in capturing the small island of Betio. The Japanese defenders, well-entrenched in their fortifications, put up a fierce resistance, inflicting heavy casualties on the landing forces.

The initial waves of Marines struggled to gain a foothold on the beach, facing a hail of machine-gun fire, mortar shells, and grenades. The landing craft, hampered by the shallow reefs surrounding the island, were unable to reach the shore, forcing the Marines to wade through waist-deep water under heavy fire.

Marines landing on Tarawa Island beach

Despite the heavy losses, the Marines persevered, pushing their way inland and gradually gaining control of the island. The fighting was intense and brutal, with close-quarters combat taking place in trenches, bunkers, and pillboxes. The Marines used flamethrowers, grenades, and explosives to clear the Japanese positions, often at great cost.

The battle for Betio raged for three days, a relentless struggle for every inch of ground. The Japanese defenders, refusing to surrender, fought to the death, their resistance fueled by a fanatical devotion to their emperor and their country.

The Battle of Tarawa was one of the bloodiest battles of the Pacific War, with heavy casualties on both sides. The U.S. Marines suffered over 3,000 casualties, including over 1,000 killed in action. The Japanese defenders were virtually annihilated, with only 17 survivors captured.

Tarawa showed that Island-Hopping would be costly—but also that the U.S. could defeat Japan's fortress islands.

▫ ***DID YOU KNOW***

- *Of the 3,636 Japanese in the garrison, only one officer and sixteen enlisted men survived. Of the 1,200 Korean laborers brought to Tarawa to construct the defenses, only 129 survived. In total, 4,690 of the island's defenders were killed.*

Flamethrower in Tarawa jungle

Battle of Kwajalein (January 31 – February 3, 1944): The First Breakthrough

Kwajalein was the largest atoll in the Marshall Islands. Its airfields and naval bases allowed Japan to launch attacks on U.S. forces. Capturing it would open the way to the Marianas and bring U.S. bombers closer to Japan.

U.S. infantry and M4 Sherman tanks attack amid the rubble of fortifications on Kwajalein on 2 February 1944

In attacking Kwajalein, the U.S. had learned from its mistakes in Tarawa, with better intelligence, a heavy pre-invasion bombardment to weaken Japanese defenses, and more effective landings to help the Marines push forward quickly. These learnings led to a devastating U.S. victory.

The battle lasted for just three days. Japan lost 7,800 men, nearly all of its defenders, while the US lost just 373 troops, showing that the U.S. was adapting to the brutal island battles.

With Kwajalein secured, the door to the Mariana Islands was open.

Battle of Saipan, Tinian, and Guam(June 15 – July 9, 1944): A Step Toward Japan Itself

The Mariana Islands, a strategically vital archipelago in the central Pacific, became a focal point of the Allied island-hopping campaign in 1944. The capture of Saipan, Tinian, and Guam, three of the largest islands in the Marianas, provided the Allies with crucial airbases for their long-range B-29 Superfortress bombers, bringing the Japanese mainland within striking distance and paving the way for the final phase of the Pacific War.

The Battle of Saipan – Hell in the Jungle

The U.S. launched one of the largest amphibious assaults of the war, with 71,000 troops. The Japanese had 31,000 defenders, well-equipped and prepared for along fight. The battle was fierce, with brutal jungle combat, artillery strikes, and hand-to-hand fighting.

As defeat became inevitable, 3,000 Japanese soldiers launched a massive Banzai charge, overwhelming U.S. positions in one final suicidal attack. The fighting was savage, with many U.S. soldiers killed before the Japanese were stopped.

Tragically, thousands of Japanese civilians, believing American soldiers would torture them, committed mass suicide by jumping off cliffs. U.S. troops watched in horror as entire families leaped to their deaths rather than surrender.

After weeks of intense fighting, the Americans secured Saipan on July 9, 1944. The victory was a significant one for the Allies, but it came at a high cost, with over 3,400 American troops killed and over 10,000 wounded, making it one of the bloodiest battles so far. The Japanese suffered even heavier losses, with nearly all of their 31,000 troops killed.

▢ ***DID YOU KNOW***

- *General Yoshitsugu Saito, the island's commander, committed suicide in his cave bunker, but not before leading the final banzai charge himself.*

The loss of Saipan led directly to the fall of Prime Minister Hideki Tojo's government in Japan. It was seen as such a devastating blow that Tojo and his cabinet resigned shortly after the battle.

The Battle of Tinian - A Swift and Decisive Victory

The Battle of Tinian, fought from July 24 to August 1, 1944, was the second major battle in the Marianas campaign. Tinian, a smaller island located just south of

Saipan, was also heavily fortified by the Japanese, with a garrison of around 8,000 troops.

The U.S. Marines, having learned from their experience on Saipan, employed a new tactic on Tinian, landing on the lightly defended northern beaches and quickly overwhelming the Japanese defenders. The fighting on Tinian was less intense than on Saipan, and the Americans secured the island within a week.

The capture of Tinian provided the Allies with another valuable airfield, which was used to launch B-29 bombing raids on Japan. The island also became a major logistics hub, supporting the Allied advance across the Pacific.

◻ **DID YOU KNOW**

- *Tinian Island, located approximately 1,500 miles south of Tokyo, was the launching point for the atomic bomb attacks against Hiroshima and Nagasaki, Japan. The Enola Gay left Tinian at 2:45 am, accompanied by two other B-29s: The Great Artiste and Necessary Evil. These planes rendezvoused over Iwo Jima and set course for Japan.*

The Battle of Guam - Reclaiming a Lost Territory

The Battle of Guam, fought from July 21 to August 10, 1944, was the final major battle in the Marianas campaign. Guam, a U.S. territory captured by the Japanese in December 1941, was a symbolic and strategic prize for the Americans.

The U.S. Marines and Army troops, supported by naval and airpower, landed on Guam on July 21, facing fierce resistance from the Japanese defenders. The fighting was intense and protracted, with heavy casualties on both sides. However, the Americans, with their superior firepower and resources, ultimately prevailed, recapturing Guam and liberating its people from Japanese occupation.

The recapture of Guam was a significant victory for the Allies, restoring American control over a strategically important territory and providing another valuable airfield for B-29 bombing raids on Japan. Guam also became a major logistics hub, supporting the Allied advance across the Pacific.

Battle of Peleliu (September 15 – November 27, 1944)

The Battle of Peleliu, part of the island-hopping campaign, was one of the bloodiest and most controversial battles of World War II. It took place on the small coral island of Peleliu in the Palau Islands and aimed to secure an airfield to support future operations in the Philippines.

However, the strategic importance of Peleliu diminished as the Allies made progress in other areas of the Pacific. The capture of the Mariana Islands in the summer of 1944 provided the Allies with airbases for their B-29 Superfortress bombers, which could reach the Japanese mainland from those islands. This reduced the need for Peleliu as a staging ground for air operations.

Despite this, the decision was made to proceed with the invasion of Peleliu. The operation was seen as a way to maintain the momentum of the Allied advance and to test new tactics and equipment in preparation for future amphibious assaults.

The invasion was notable for a drastic change in Japanese defensive tactics, resulting in the highest casualty rate amongst US forces in an amphibious operation during the Pacific War.

Amphibious trac coming out of a Landing Ship, Tank (LST), Peleliu beach

In a departure from the Japanese strategy in previous island battles such as Tarawa and Saipan, where defending IJA troops intensely contested the landing beaches but not the island interior. On Peleliu the Japanese constructed extensive fortifications, caves and tunnels within the ridges that dominated the center of the island, called The Umurbrogol Pocket, creating a formidable stronghold. This was an example of fukkaku, or honeycomb, tactics that Japanese island garrisons would again utilize during the battles of Iwo Jima and Okinawa in 1945.

The U.S. Marines, facing a determined and well-equipped enemy, struggled to make headway in the Umurbrogol Pocket. The fighting was particularly intense and costly, with heavy casualties on both sides. The Marines used flamethrowers, grenades, and explosives to clear the Japanese positions, but the defenders, using their knowledge of the terrain and their interconnected network of tunnels, were able to resist for weeks.

The battle for the Umurbrogol Pocket was a grueling test of endurance for the Marines, who faced not only the enemy but also the challenges of the terrain, the heat, and the constant threat of disease. The fighting continued until late November 1944, when the last Japanese defenders were finally overcome.

Instead of the predicted four days, it took over two months and over 10,000 casualties, including 2,300 killed, for American forces to secure the island!

The Battle of Peleliu was not only a bloody and costly battle but also a controversial one as the strategic necessity of the operation was questioned.

◻ DID YOU KNOW

- *Peleliu had the highest casualty rate of any amphibious assault in the Pacific War. The 1st Marine Division suffered 6,526 casualties, nearly a third of its entire force.*

- *The island was a barren, rocky hellscape with temperatures exceeding 115°F (46°C). U.S. troops ran out of water, and what they did have was often contaminated with fuel or saltwater.*

- *Even after the island was officially captured, a small group of Japanese soldiers refused to surrender and remained hidden until April 1947, two years after the war ended.*

The high casualty rate on Peleliu, particularly among the Marines, also raised concerns about the cost of victory in the Pacific War. Some critics argued that the battle was unnecessary and that the lives lost could have been spared.

The Battle for the Philippines: MacArthur's Return (October 1944 – August 1945)

The islands, occupied by Japan since 1942, were a vital stepping stone for the Allies in their island-hopping campaign towards the Japanese home islands. The liberation of the Philippines would not only restore American control over a strategically important territory but also cut off Japan's access to vital resources in Southeast Asia, further isolating it and weakening its war effort.

For Japan, the Philippines represented a crucial defensive line, protecting its access to oil, rubber, and other raw materials from Southeast Asia. The loss of the Philippines would be a devastating blow to Japan's war effort, hindering its ability to sustain its military operations and defend its home islands.

Let's look at two critical events in the liberation of the Philippines – the invasion of Leyte and the Battle of Leyte Gulf.

The Invasion of Leyte (October 20, 1944): The Return Begins

The liberation of the Philippines began with the invasion of Leyte, the most strategically important island in the archipelago.

Launched on October 20, 1944, this was the largest amphibious assault in the Pacific, with over 200,000 U.S. troops, supported by a massive naval fleet.

The Japanese defenders were well dug in, but they were outgunned and outnumbered. Within days, U.S. forces had established a firm beachhead.

After the initial assault, MacArthur waded ashore in full uniform, flanked by his officers. This hugely symbolic moment was broadcast across the world, fulfilling his promise from 1942. Speaking into a microphone, he addressed the Filipino people, urging them to rise up and fight alongside the Americans.

General Douglas MacArthur wades ashore during initial landings at Leyte, Philippine Islands.

Even before the U.S. arrived, Filipino guerrillas had been fighting a brutal war against Japanese occupation. MacArthur's return inspired an uprising, with resistance fighters attacking Japanese positions from the jungles and villages.

The Battle of Leyte Gulf (October 23–26, 1944)

The Battle of Leyte Gulf was fought in the swirling waters around the Philippine island of Leyte. It was a battle for the strategic heart of the Philippines, and was fought to prevent Japanese reinforcements from disrupting the land campaign.

The strategic stakes of the Battle of Leyte Gulf were high, and both sides committed their remaining naval power to the fight, determined to secure victory, regardless of the cost.

By October 1944, the war in the Pacific had turned against Japan. The U.S. had island-hopped across the Pacific, capturing Guam, Saipan, and the Philippines, putting American bombers within range of Japan's homeland. The Japanese Navy was severely weakened, but they still had one last desperate chance to turn the tide. If they could destroy the American fleet at Leyte Gulf, they could cripple the U.S. invasion of the Philippines and buy time for Japan to regroup.

This battle was Japan's last stand on the seas - and they were willing to use every tactic imaginable, even suicide attacks, to achieve victory.

◻ **DID YOU KNOW**

- *Leyte Gulf was the largest naval battle ever fought, involving nearly 300 ships and over 200,000 sailors.*

The Battle Unfolds: A Multi-Pronged Assault

The Battle of Leyte Gulf was a complex engagement, involving a series of battles fought over several days in different parts of Leyte Gulf. The Japanese, under the overall command of Admiral Soemu Toyoda, launched a multi-pronged attack, hoping to surprise and overwhelm the American forces.

The Japanese knew they couldn't defeat the U.S. in a direct fight, so they devised a bold and risky strategy:

1. **Decoy Force (Admiral Ozawa)**. Japan sent a small carrier force north to lure Admiral Halsey's powerful U.S. carriers away.

2. **Southern Force (Admiral Nishimura and Shima)**. They would attack from the south to break through American defenses.

3. **Central Force (Admiral Kurita)**. The main fleet, including Yamato, would slip through the middle and destroy the U.S. landing forces at Leyte Gulf

If it worked, they could wipe out thousands of U.S. troops and ships.

But everything went wrong!

The Four Major Battles of Leyte Gulf

1. The Battle of the Sibuyan Sea (October 24, 1944) – The Death of Musashi

The Japanese Central Force entered the Sibuyan Sea, heading straight for Leyte. U.S. aircraft from Admiral Halsey's carriers spotted them and launched wave after wave of attacks. The massive battleship Musashi, sister ship to the Yamato, was hit by 19 torpedoes and 17 bombs, sinking under a fiery explosion. Kurita retreated temporarily, but later continued toward Leyte Gulf.

2. The Battle of Surigao Strait (October 25, 1944) – A Deadly Ambush

Japan's Southern Force sailed into a trap. U.S. battleships and cruisers, waiting in the strait, unleashed a devastating ambush, sinking several Japanese ships. Nishimura's fleet was wiped out in one of the last battleship-on-battleship clashes in history.

3. The Battle off Cape Engaño (October 25, 1944) – The Japanese Decoy Works...Too Well

Japan's decoy force, with its small number of aircraft carriers, successfully lured Admiral Halsey north. Halsey's ships chased and sank all four Japanese carriers. But by the time Halsey realized his mistake, the real Japanese attack force (Central Force) was already approaching Leyte Gulf.

4. The Battle off Samar (October 25, 1944) – The "Taffy 3" Miracle

With Halsey's carriers gone, Japan's powerful Central Force had a clear shot at the vulnerable U.S. landing force. Only a small group of escort carriers ("Taffy 3") and destroyers stood in their way. Outnumbered and outgunned, the U.S. ships fought with incredible bravery, launching desperate torpedo attacks and setting smoke screens. The Japanese fleet, confused and battered, retreated. Against all odds, the U.S. held the line and saved the invasion force.

The Kamikaze Attacks: Japan's New, Terrifying Weapon

For the first time in history, Japan launched large-scale kamikaze (suicide) attacks. This involved hundreds of pilots, who volunteered to crash their planes into U.S. ships. Ships like USS St. Lo, USS Franklin, and others were struck by kamikazes, causing massive damage and killed thousands of sailors.

While terrifying, the kamikaze attacks failed to stop the U.S. Navy's advance.

The Aftermath: The End of the Japanese Navy

By October 26, 1944, the Battle of Leyte Gulf was over.

Japan had lost 26 ships, including four aircraft carriers and the battleship Musashi, and was effectively destroyed as a coherent fighting force and could no longer conduct major offensive operations. From this point on, Japan could no longer fight a full-scale naval war.

The victory led to the eventual liberation of the Philippines, and was the beginning of the end for Japan - and a preview of the brutal battles still to come.

Liberation - A Long and Bloody Campaign

- Japan refused to surrender the Philippines easily. The battles dragged on for months, with some of the fiercest fighting taking place in:

   Leyte (October–December 1944) with over 70,000 Japanese troops killed.

- **Luzon (January–August 1945)**, the largest and most strategically important island in the Philippines, the location of the capital, Manila. This was the largest battle, with an invasion force larger than D-Day, with over 175,000 troops. U.S. troops landed with little initial resistance, as the Japanese had withdrawn to defensive positions inland. Japanese kamikaze aircraft launched devastating attacks on U.S. ships, damaging or sinking several vessels. Around 230,000 Japanese troops died (many from starvation and disease), and 10,300 Americans.

- **Manila (February–March 1945).** After securing Lingayen Gulf, U.S. forces pushed south toward Manila. Japanese naval forces, under Rear Admiral Sanji Iwabuchi, refused to abandon Manila and turned it into a fortress, turning the battle into an horrific urban battle. Japanese troops, trapped in the city, brutalized civilians, committing massacres, rape, and arson, resulting in over 100,000 Filipino deaths. U.S. and Filipino forces fought street by street, using tanks, artillery, and flamethrowers to root out the Japanese defenders. The intense fighting devastated Manila, reducing much of the city to rubble. By March 3, 1945, Manila was finally liberated, but at an horrific cost.

While the Allies had largely gained control of key strategic points on Luzon by March 1945, pockets of Japanese resistance continued to fight in mountainous areas until the war's end. It was until September 2, 1945, that Japan surrendered in the Philippines, 1 day after Japan had officially surrendered. The staggering cost of liberation was:

- Over 250,000 Japanese soldiers dead.

- About 50,000 American troops dead or wounded.

- An estimated 1 million Filipino civilians dead from war, starvation, or massacres.

Despite the losses, the return of MacArthur had a powerful symbolic and strategic impact. It fulfilled America's promise to its Filipino allies. It crippled Japan's hold in the Pacific, cutting off their supply lines, and it brought the U.S. one step closer to Japan.

☐ *DID YOU KNOW*

- *The Battle of Manila is often referred to as "the Stalingrad of Asia" and widely considered to be one of the most intense and worst urban battles ever fought.*

For the Filipino people, MacArthur became a symbol of resilience and liberation. He was honored as a national hero, and his role in freeing the Philippines was forever remembered. After securing the Philippines, the U.S. turned its attention to Iwo Jima and Okinawa- the last major battles before Japan itself.

CHAPTER 13: THE BRITISH CAMPAIGN IN BURMA

The Burma Campaign, a grueling and often overlooked theater of World War II, was fought in the dense jungles and rugged mountains of Southeast Asia. This campaign, waged primarily by British and Indian forces against the Imperial Japanese Army, was fought in one of the most challenging environments of the war.

Geography: A Land of Jungle and Mountains

Burma, now known as Myanmar, is a country of diverse geography, characterized by dense jungles, rugged mountains, and fertile river valleys. The country's terrain played a crucial role in the Burma Campaign, shaping the tactics employed by both sides and influencing the course of the conflict.

The dense jungles of Burma, with their limited visibility and treacherous terrain, favored guerrilla warfare and ambushes. The Japanese, skilled in jungle warfare, used the terrain to their advantage, infiltrating behind enemy lines and launching surprise attacks on Allied forces.

The mountainous regions of Burma also presented challenges for both sides. The steep slopes, narrow passes, and limited road networks made movement difficult and logistical support a nightmare. The mountains also provided natural defensive positions, which both sides exploited to their advantage.

Resources: A Prize Worth Fighting For

Burma was also rich in natural resources, including oil, timber, minerals, and agricultural products. These resources were strategically important for both the Allies and Japan, making Burma a valuable prize worth fighting for.

For Japan, capturing Burma would secure its eastern flank, protecting its conquests in Southeast Asia from potential Allied counterattacks. It would also provide access to Burma's valuable resources, particularly oil, which was essential for Japan's war effort.

Allied Strategy: Protecting India and Supporting China

The Allied strategy in Burma was twofold: to protect India from a potential Japanese invasion and to maintain a supply route to China. India, the "jewel in the crown" of the British Empire, was a vital asset for the Allies, providing manpower, resources, and a strategic base for operations in Southeast Asia.

The Burma Road, a 700-mile highway connecting Lashio in Burma to Kunming in China, was a crucial lifeline for China's Nationalist government during the Second Sino-Japanese War. The road, built in the 1930s, allowed the Allies to transport supplies, weapons, and ammunition to China, supporting its resistance against Japanese aggression.

The Allies, recognizing the strategic importance of Burma, deployed a substantial force of British, Indian, and Commonwealth troops to defend the colony and keep the Burma Road open. However, the initial Allied efforts in Burma were hampered by a lack of preparation for jungle warfare, inadequate equipment, and poor leadership.

Japanese Success

The early stages of the British Campaign in Burma were marked by a series of disheartening setbacks and a grueling retreat for the Allied forces. The Japanese, with their superior tactics, experience in jungle warfare, and relentless offensive, quickly overran British defenses, capturing key cities and strategic locations. The fall of Rangoon, the capital of Burma, and the subsequent retreat of British forces into India exposed the vulnerabilities of the Allied forces and the challenges they faced in adapting to the harsh realities of the Southeast Asian theater.

The British, preoccupied with the war in Europe and underestimating the Japanese threat, were ill-prepared for the defense of Burma. The British forces in Burma, consisting of British, Indian, and Burmese troops, were outnumbered and outgunned by the Japanese, and they lacked the training and equipment necessary for jungle warfare.

The Japanese Invasion: A Swift and Decisive Offensive

The Japanese invasion of Burma began in January 1942, with a force of around 35,000 troops from the 15th Army, commanded by Lieutenant General Shojiro Iida. The Japanese, employing their experience in jungle warfare and their superior tactics, quickly overran British defenses, capturing key towns and strategic locations.

The Fall of Rangoon: A Strategic Blow

The fall of Rangoon in March 1942 was a major strategic blow to the Allies. The city, the capital of Burma and a major port, was a vital hub for trade and communication, and its capture by the Japanese disrupted Allied supply lines and threatened India's eastern border.

The loss of Rangoon also had a demoralizing effect on the British and Indian troops, who had been forced to retreat in the face of the Japanese advance. The fall of the capital city raised questions about the British ability to defend its colonies and its commitment to the war effort in Asia.

The Retreat to India: A Grueling Ordeal

The fall of Rangoon was followed by a chaotic and grueling retreat by British and Indian forces into India. The retreat, which covered over 1,000 miles through dense jungle and mountainous terrain, was one of the longest and most arduous retreats in British military history.

The retreating troops faced numerous challenges, including disease, starvation, and the constant threat of attack by Japanese forces. The monsoon season, with its torrential rains and flooding, further hampered the retreat, turning the journey into a nightmare of mud, exhaustion, and despair.

Despite these hardships, the British and Indian forces managed to reach India, though with heavy losses and a significant loss of morale. The retreat to India marked a low point for the Allies in the Burma campaign, but it also served as a learning experience, highlighting the need for better training, equipment, and leadership for jungle warfare.

The Road to Liberation (January 1944 – November 1994)

The tide of the Burma Campaign began to turn in 1944, as the Allies, under the leadership of General William Slim, launched a series of successful counteroffensives that pushed back the Japanese and ultimately liberated Burma. Let's explore the key turning points in the Burma Campaign, the Battles of Kohima and Imphal, the Allied counteroffensive, and the factors that contributed to the Allied victory.

The Japanese Offensive: A Bold Gamble

In early 1944, the Japanese, under the command of Lieutenant General Renya Mutaguchi, launched a major offensive into India, aiming to capture the strategically important towns of Imphal and Kohima and disrupt Allied supply lines to China. The offensive, codenamed Operation U-Go, was a bold gamble by the Japanese, who were hoping to exploit the perceived weakness of the Allied forces in the region and achieve a decisive victory that would force the British to negotiate a peace settlement.

The Japanese offensive, however, faced numerous challenges. The terrain, the climate, and the logistical difficulties of operating in a remote and mountainous region all hampered the Japanese advance. Moreover, the Allied forces, under the leadership of General William Slim, had been reorganized and reinforced, and they were better prepared to resist the Japanese onslaught.

The Battle of Kohima (April-June 1944): A Crucial Stand

The Battle of Kohima, fought from April to June 1944, was a crucial turning point in the Burma Campaign. The town of Kohima, located on a strategic ridge overlooking the Imphal Plain, was a vital supply point for the Allied forces defending Imphal.

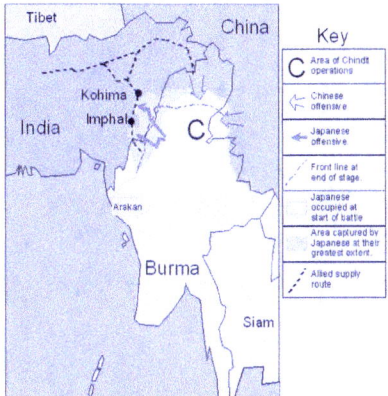

Imphal and Kohima campaign.

The Japanese launched a fierce assault on the town, surrounding it and besieging the small garrison of British and Indian troops. The defenders, outnumbered and outgunned, fought with extraordinary courage and tenacity, repelling wave after wave of Japanese attacks.

Indian and Gurkha soldiers inspect captured Japanese ordnance, Imphal-Kohima battle, 1944

The battle for Kohima was a close-quarters struggle, with hand-to-hand combat taking place in trenches, bunkers, and even on the tennis court of the Deputy Commissioner's bungalow! The defenders, facing dwindling supplies and ammunition, held their ground, inflicting heavy casualties on the Japanese and preventing them from capturing the town.

The arrival of reinforcements in May 1944, including tanks and artillery, allowed the Allies to launch a counterattack, pushing back the Japanese and breaking the siege of Kohima.

The Battle of Kohima was a costly victory for the Allies, but it was also a crucial one.

The Battle of Imphal (March-July 1944): A Strategic Victory

The Battle of Imphal, fought from March to July 1944, was another key turning point in the Burma Campaign. Imphal, the capital of Manipur state in India, was a strategically important town that controlled access to the Assam region and the vital supply route to China.

The Japanese, aiming to capture Imphal and disrupt the Allied supply lines, launched a major offensive against the town, surrounding it and besieging the British and Indian forces defending it. The defenders were again outnumbered but, this time, well-supplied, fought with determination, repelling the Japanese attacks and inflicting heavy casualties.

The battle for Imphal was a protracted and bloody struggle, with both sides facing challenges of terrain, climate, and logistics. The monsoon season, with its torrential rains and flooding, further hampered the fighting, making movement and supply difficult for both sides.

Despite these challenges, the Allied forces were able to hold their ground and inflict heavy losses on the Japanese. The arrival of reinforcements and the effective use of air power allowed the Allies to launch a counteroffensive, pushing back the Japanese and breaking the siege of Imphal.

Men of the Devonshire Regiment sign their autographs on Japanese flags captured at Nippon Ridge during the Battle of Imphal-Kohima.

The Battle of Imphal was a strategic victory for the Allies, demonstrating their ability to defeat the Japanese in a major offensive and paved the way for their counteroffensive into Burma.

The Allied Counteroffensive: Liberating Burma

Following the victories at Kohima and Imphal, the Allies launched a major counteroffensive into Burma, aiming to liberate the country from Japanese occupation and reopen the Burma Road. The counteroffensive, led by General Slim, was characterized by its innovative tactics, its effective use of air power, and the close cooperation between British, Indian, and Commonwealth forces.

Slim's strategy involved a series of flanking maneuvers and bold advances, exploiting the Japanese weaknesses and their overextended supply lines. The Allies also made effective use of air power, dropping supplies to their troops and attacking Japanese positions.

The Allied counteroffensive was a success, gradually pushing back the Japanese and liberating key towns and strategic locations. The capture of Mandalay in March 1945 and Rangoon in May 1945 marked the culmination of the Allied campaign in Burma, effectively ending the Japanese occupation and reopening the Burma Road.

☐ **DID YOU KNOW**

- *The Japanese surrendered in Burma on August 28, 1945, at a ceremony in Rangoon, two weeks after Emperor Hirohito had announced Japan's surrender.*

Role of Field Marshal William Slim

Let's explore the key role played by General Slim in the Burma Campaign, his leadership, innovative tactics, and lasting legacy.

Leadership: Inspiring Confidence and Resilience

Field Marshal William Slim, a veteran of World War I and a seasoned commander, took command of the British Fourteenth Army in Burma in late 1943. The Fourteenth Army, a diverse force composed of British, Indian, and Commonwealth troops, had suffered heavy losses and demoralizing defeats in the early stages of the Burma Campaign.

Slim, recognizing the challenges facing his troops, focused on rebuilding their morale and instilling a sense of confidence and purpose. He emphasized the importance of training, discipline, and esprit de corps, fostering a sense of camaraderie and shared purpose among his diverse force.

Slim's leadership style was characterized by his humility, his empathy for his troops, and his ability to inspire trust and loyalty. He was known for his down-to-earth approach, his willingness to share the hardships of his men, and his ability to communicate effectively with soldiers from all ranks and backgrounds.

Field Marshal Sir William Slim, chatting with a Gurkha rifleman, Burma, November 1944.

Slim's leadership was crucial in transforming the Fourteenth Army from a demoralized and defeated force into a confident and victorious one. He inspired his troops to overcome the challenges of the Burma Campaign, to fight with courage and determination, and to ultimately achieve victory against a formidable enemy.

Innovative Tactics: Adapting to the Jungle

Field Marshal Slim was not only a skilled leader but also a brilliant tactician. He recognized the need to adapt Allied tactics to the unique challenges of the Burma theater, where the dense jungles, rugged mountains, and monsoon rains made conventional warfare difficult and costly.

Slim's innovative tactics included:

- Emphasis on Jungle Warfare Training: Slim recognized that the Fourteenth Army lacked the training and experience necessary for fighting in the jungles of Burma. He implemented a rigorous training program that focused on jungle survival skills, patrolling, ambushing, and other tactics suited to the terrain and the enemy.

- Developing Flexibility and Mobility: Slim emphasized the importance of flexibility and mobility in jungle warfare, recognizing that the Japanese were skilled in infiltration and encirclement tactics. He reorganized the Fourteenth Army into smaller, more mobile units, capable of operating independently and adapting to the changing battlefield conditions.

- Effective Use of Air Supply: Slim also recognized the importance of air supply in overcoming the logistical challenges of the Burma theater. He established a system of air supply that allowed his troops to operate deep behind enemy lines without relying on vulnerable road networks. This innovative use of air power gave the Fourteenth Army a significant advantage over the Japanese, who were heavily reliant on road transport for their supplies.

Slim's innovative tactics were crucial in turning the tide of the Burma Campaign. His emphasis on jungle warfare training, flexibility, mobility, and the effective use of air supply allowed the Fourteenth Army to overcome the challenges of the terrain and the enemy, ultimately leading to victory.

A Master of Jungle Warfare

Field Marshal Slim's leadership and innovative tactics earned him a reputation as one of the most skilled and respected British generals of World War II. He is often referred to as the "forgotten victor" of the war, as his achievements in Burma were overshadowed by the more prominent campaigns in Europe and the Pacific.

However, Slim's legacy as a master of jungle warfare and a brilliant military leader is undeniable. His contributions to the Allied victory in Burma were significant, and his leadership and tactics continue to be studied and admired by military professionals around the world.

Slim's legacy also extends beyond the battlefield. He was a strong advocate for the welfare of his troops, and he emphasized the importance of treating all soldiers, regardless of their background or rank, with respect and dignity. He was also a vocal critic of racism and discrimination, and he championed the cause of Indian independence after the war.

Slim's legacy is one of leadership, innovation, and compassion. He was a true hero of the Burma Campaign, and his contributions to the Allied victory should never be forgotten.

▢ **DID YOU KNOW**

- *The British Fourteenth Army, a multinational force composed of British, Indian, African, and Chinese troops, was often referred to as the "Forgotten Army" because the European and Pacific theaters overshadowed its achievements. Despite this, it was one of the largest Allied land forces of the war.*
- *A U.S. special forces unit, Merrill's Marauders, operated deep behind enemy lines in Burma with no conventional supply lines. The unit endured extreme exhaustion, disease, and malnutrition while achieving remark-*

able victories, particularly at Myitkyina.

Harsh Conditions

The Burma Campaign was not only a test of military strategy and tactics but also a grueling battle against the harsh realities of the environment. The soldiers who fought in Burma faced a relentless onslaught of challenges, from the dense jungles and rugged mountains to the debilitating diseases and the constant threat of starvation. Let's look at the harsh conditions that made the Burma Campaign one of the most challenging and demanding theaters of World War II.

Jungle Warfare: A Battle Against Nature

Burma's jungles were a relentless adversary, with dense vegetation, stifling heat, and rampant disease testing soldiers' endurance. Limited visibility created constant fear, while thick undergrowth and rough terrain slowed movement and disrupted supply lines. Disease-carrying insects spread malaria and dengue, further weakening troops already strained by combat. The soldiers, already weakened by the harsh conditions and the stress of combat, were particularly vulnerable to these diseases.

The jungle warfare in Burma was a grueling and psychologically demanding experience. The soldiers had to adapt to a new kind of warfare, one that relied on stealth, cunning, and the ability to endure extreme physical and mental hardship.

Disease: A Constant Threat

Disease was a relentless threat in Burma, worsened by the tropical climate, poor sanitation, and limited medical care. Malaria, the most widespread illness, caused fever, chills, and weakness, severely affecting Allied troops. Dysentery, fueled by unclean water and contaminated food, led to severe dehydration, while constant exposure to heat and moisture caused skin infections. These illnesses drained soldiers' strength, impaired combat effectiveness, and eroded morale.

Malnutrition: A Slow and Insidious Killer

Malnutrition was a severe challenge in Burma due to supply difficulties and disrupted food production. Soldiers survived on inadequate rations, leading to weakness, disease susceptibility, and reduced combat effectiveness. The gradual effects—fatigue, cognitive decline, and depression—further impaired their ability to fight and recover.

Isolation: A Psychological Challenge

The Burma Campaign was marked by extreme isolation. Soldiers, stationed in remote jungles, were cut off from loved ones and familiar comforts. The lack of communication, constant danger, and absence of support took a heavy toll, leading to loneliness, depression, and anxiety, making it harder to cope with the stresses of war.

Impact of the Japanese Retreat

The Allied victory in the Burma Campaign was a hard-won triumph, a testament to the resilience and adaptability of the British and Indian forces who fought against a formidable enemy in one of the most challenging theaters of World War II. The Japanese retreat from Burma in 1945 marked a significant turning point in the war in Southeast Asia, with far-reaching consequences for the region and the global balance of power. This section explores the impact of the Japanese retreat from Burma, highlighting the collapse of the Japanese position in Southeast Asia, the reopening of vital supply lines to China, and the inspiration it provided for Allied morale.

The Collapse of the Japanese Position in Southeast Asia

The Japanese retreat from Burma marked the beginning of the end for their ambitions in Southeast Asia, and exposed the overextension and vulnerability of the Japanese Empire. Losing this strategic territory cut off access to vital resources and weakened their defensive perimeter, leaving their conquests vulnerable. Heavy losses and harsh conditions also drained morale, reinforcing the growing sense that Japan's defeat was inevitable.

Reopening Supply Lines to China: A Lifeline Restored

The liberation of Burma allowed the Allies to reopen the Burma Road, a crucial supply route to China that had been cut off since 1942. This restored the flow of weapons and supplies to China's Nationalist forces, bolstering their resistance against Japan. It also enabled troop movements and closer coordination between Allied forces in China and Southeast Asia. The road's reopening tied down Japanese troops and reinforced China's role as a key Allied partner in the war.

Inspiration for Allied Morale: A Symbol of Resilience

The Allied victory in Burma and the subsequent Japanese retreat had a profound impact on Allied morale. It had been a long and arduous struggle, but victory was a morale booster, particularly the British and Indian troops who had endured the hardships of the campaign. It also inspired confidence among the civilian populations of the Allied nations, demonstrating that the tide of the war was turning in their favor.

CHAPTER 14: THE BATTLE OF IWO JIMA (FEB 19 – MARCH 26, 1945)

By early 1945, the war in the Pacific was entering its final phase. The Philippines had been liberated, the Japanese Navy was destroyed, and Allied forces were steadily advancing towards the Japanese home islands. In this desperate situation, Iwo Jima, a small volcanic island located just 750 miles from Tokyo, took on a crucial strategic significance for the Japanese.

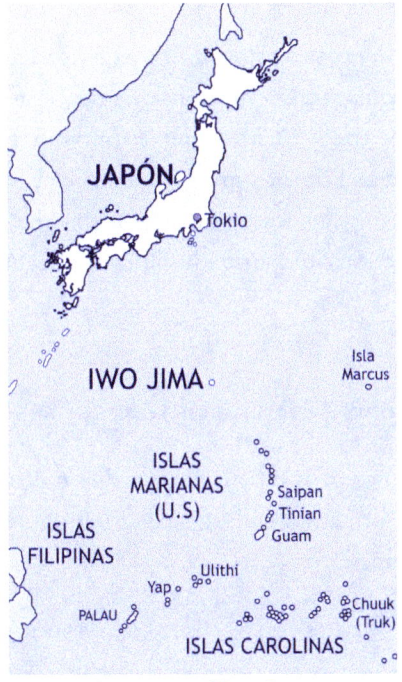

Location of Iwo Jima

The Japanese objectives for Iwo Jima were primarily defensive. Iwo Jima, with its radar installations and airfields, served as an early warning station for the Japanese mainland, providing crucial intelligence about approaching American bombers. The Japanese also hoped to inflict heavy casualties on the American forces, aiming to demoralize them and delay their advance towards the Japanese home islands. The island's defenses were designed to make any invasion a costly and bloody affair, potentially buying time for Japan to prepare for a final defense of its homeland. The Japanese also saw the defense of Iwo Jima as a way to demonstrate their resolve and determination to fight to the death, even in the face of overwhelming odds.

They hoped that this display of fanaticism would demoralize the Americans and weaken their will to continue the war.

Allied Objectives: A Stepping Stone and a Lifeline

For the Allies, Iwo Jima could act as an Emergency Landing Strip for B-29s which often suffered damage on its missions over the Japanese mainland. It could also serve as a base for the P-51 Mustang, a long-range fighter, which could operate from Iwo Jima and provide protection for the bombers, increasing their effectiveness and reducing their losses. And capturing the island would eliminate Japanese radar installations and airfields, allowing the Allies to operate more freely in the region.

The Island's Geography: A Natural Fortress

The strategic importance of Iwo Jima was further enhanced by its geography. The island, a volcanic formation with rugged terrain, provided natural defensive advantages for the Japanese.

The most prominent feature of Iwo Jima was Mount Suribachi, a dormant volcano that dominated the southern end of the island. The Japanese had fortified Mount Suribachi with a network of tunnels, caves, and bunkers, making it a formidable stronghold.

The island's surface was covered in volcanic ash, which made movement difficult for troops and vehicles. The terrain was also rugged and uneven, providing natural cover for the Japanese defenders and making it difficult for the Americans to maneuver and deploy their firepower effectively.

The Japanese had constructed an elaborate network of underground tunnels and caves throughout the island, connecting their defensive positions and allowing them to move troops and supplies undetected. These underground defenses made it difficult for the Americans to pinpoint and eliminate Japanese positions, prolonging the battle and increasing casualties.

☐ DID YOU KNOW

- *Iwo Jima is a volcanic island with no rivers, lakes, or natural freshwater sources. Both American and Japanese troops had to rely on transported or desalinated water. The Japanese had to collect rainwater in cisterns, while the U.S. Navy shipped water in from nearby islands.*

- *Iwo Jima was a sulfuric volcanic island, and the air was filled with the stench of sulfur. Many Marines described it as smelling like "rotten eggs," which added to the hellish conditions. The name "Iwo Jima" even translates to "Sulfur Island."*

The Human Cost: A Battle of Attrition

The Battle of Iwo Jima was a brutal and costly struggle, with heavy casualties on both sides. The Americans, despite their superior firepower and resources, faced a determined and resourceful enemy who was willing to fight to the death.

The Japanese defenders, entrenched in their fortifications and underground defenses, inflicted heavy losses on the American attackers. The fighting was often hand-to-hand, with soldiers battling in trenches, bunkers, and caves, using flamethrowers, grenades, and bayonets.

The battle lasted for 36 days, a grueling test of endurance and courage for both sides. The Americans ultimately prevailed, capturing Iwo Jima and raising the American flag on Mount Suribachi in a moment that became a symbol of American resilience and victory.

However, that victory came at a high cost. The Americans suffered over 26,000 casualties, including nearly 7,000 killed in action. The Japanese suffered even heavier losses, with nearly all of their 21,000 defenders killed.

The Japanese Defenders: Dug-in and Determined

Iwo Jima was unlike any other battle in the Pacific. The Japanese did not defend the beaches—instead, they built a network of tunnels, bunkers, and hidden artillery positions.

21,000 Japanese soldiers, commanded by General Tadamichi Kuribayashi, were dug in across the island. They built 11 miles of tunnels, with bunkers buried deep underground, making traditional bombing raids nearly useless. There would be no Banzai charges—only methodical, calculated, brutal resistance.

Marines in front of a Japanese cave dug into the rock

Kuribayashi's plan was simple: Make the Americans pay for every inch of ground with blood.

The U.S. Marines: Island Hopping Veterans

The U.S. Marines were the primary assault force in the Battle of Iwo Jima. These battle-hardened veterans, having fought in numerous island-hopping campaigns across the Pacific, were well-equipped and experienced in amphibious warfare. They were also highly motivated, driven by a sense of duty, patriotism, and a desire to avenge the losses suffered at Pearl Harbor and other battles.

The Marines were organized into three divisions: the 3rd, 4th, and 5th Marine Divisions, comprising a total of approximately 70,000 troops. They were supported by a massive naval and air contingent, including battleships, aircraft carriers, cruisers, destroyers, and hundreds of aircraft.

The Marines were equipped with the latest weaponry and technology, including flamethrowers, bazookas, and amphibious tractors (LVTs), which allowed them to overcome the challenges of the island's terrain and the Japanese defenses. They also benefited from extensive training and preparation, having learned from their experiences in previous battles and adapted their tactics to the unique challenges of Iwo Jima.

Key Phases of the Battle

Pre-Battle Bombardment: Softening the Island

In the days leading up to the invasion of Iwo Jima, the U.S. Navy unleashed a massive bombardment of the island, aiming to soften its defenses and weaken the Japanese resistance. Battleships, cruisers, and destroyers pounded the island with their heavy guns, while carrier-based aircraft dropped bombs and strafed enemy positions.

The bombardment was intended to destroy Japanese fortifications, disrupt their communication lines, and demoralize the defenders. However, the Japanese, anticipating the invasion, had constructed their network of underground tunnels and bunkers, protecting them from the brunt of the bombardment.

While the bombardment did cause some damage to the island's defenses, it also alerted the Japanese to the impending invasion, giving them time to prepare for the American assault.

Amphibious Landings: Storming the Beaches

On February 19, 1945, the first wave of 30,000 U.S. Marines launched their amphibious assault on Iwo Jima. Instead of immediate resistance, they were met with silence. But as the Navy bombardment stopped and the Marines filled the beaches, the Japanese sprang their trap - machine guns, mortars, and artillery erupted from hidden positions.

Marines bound for Iwo Jima

Within the first day, over 2,400 Marines were killed or wounded.

The sand was so soft that it swallowed Marines' boots, making it nearly impossible to run. They had nowhere to take cover, and the Japanese fired from invisible tunnels and caves.

Despite the heavy losses, the Marines persevered, pushing their way inland and gradually establishing a beachhead. The fighting was intense and brutal, with close-quarters combat taking place in trenches, bunkers, and caves.

The Marines used flamethrowers, grenades, and explosives to clear the Japanese positions, often at great cost. The Japanese defenders, entrenched in their fortifications, fought with a tenacity that shocked and demoralized the American attackers.

Securing Mount Suribachi: A Symbolic Victory

The first major objective was Mount Suribachi, the highest point on the island. From here, the Japanese could see everything below and fire at will on the landing forces. For four days, Marines fought their way up the volcanic slopes, using flamethrowers and grenades to clear out tunnels.

On the morning of February 23, a patrol of Marines from Easy Company, 2nd Battalion, 28th Marines, reached the summit of Mount Suribachi and raised the American flag, a moment captured in the iconic photograph by Joe Rosenthal.

Raising the Flag on Iwo Jima

◻ **DID YOU KNOW**

- *The image became a symbol of American courage and sacrifice. However, three of the six men in the photo would die before the battle was over.*

Prolonged Fighting: A Grueling Test of Endurance

While the flag-raising boosted morale, the battle was far from over. The real fight was across the island, where thousands of Japanese soldiers were waiting in fortified bunkers. The Marines advanced inch by inch, facing constant sniper fire and deadly ambushes. The Japanese never surrendered, forcing U.S. forces to clear every bunker, one by one.

By the time Iwo Jima was officially declared secure on March 26, 1945, nearly 7,000 U.S. Marines were dead, and over 20,000 were wounded.

Only 216 Japanese soldiers were captured alive - the rest fought to the death.

▫ **DID YOU KNOW**

- *Iwo Jima became one of the deadliest battles in U.S. Marine Corps history. One-third of all Marines killed in WWII died on Iwo Jima.*

- *The psychological toll was enormous, as many survivors suffered from PTSD and survivor's guilt.*

After its capture, Iwo Jima became a critical base for U.S. bombers. It is estimated that over 2,200 B-29s made emergency landings on Iwo Jima during the war, saving the lives of thousands of airmen.

For the Marines, Iwo Jima was a brutal reminder that the closer they got to Japan, the deadlier the war became, and crucially for American military planners, an horrific preview of what an invasion of Japan would look like. It led directly to the decision to use atomic bombs to force Japan's surrender.

CHAPTER 15: THE BATTLE OF OKINAWA (MARCH 26 – SEPT 7, 1945)

Okinawa was the last major battle of World War II and one of the bloodiest and most significant conflicts in the Pacific Theater.

Okinawa, the largest of the Ryukyu Islands, was just 340 miles from mainland Japan, with four airfields, making it an ideal launch point for the planned invasion of Japan (Operation Downfall).

The capture of Okinawa, so close to the Japanese mainland, would also have a significant psychological impact on the Japanese people and military, demonstrating the Allies' determination and capability to invade the heart of Japan. This psychological pressure was seen as a potential factor in forcing Japan's surrender, and avoiding a costly and bloody invasion of the home islands.

For Japan, Okinawa was the last line of defense before the home islands, and its defense was seen as crucial. If the U.S. took the island, the Japanese homeland would be within bombing and invasion range. Thus, the Japanese defenders were ordered to fight to the death.

The Battle of Okinawa was a brutal and costly struggle, with heavy casualties on both sides. The Americans, despite their superior firepower and resources, faced a determined and resourceful enemy, entrenched in their fortifications and underground defenses, who was willing to fight to the death. The fighting was often hand-to-hand, with soldiers battling in trenches, bunkers, and caves, using flamethrowers, grenades, and bayonets.

The battle lasted for 82 days. The Americans ultimately prevailed, capturing Okinawa and securing a strategically important victory for the Allies.

However, the victory came at a high cost. The Americans suffered over 49,000 casualties, including over 12,000 killed in action. The Japanese suffered even heavier losses, with an estimated 100,000 soldiers killed and tens of thousands of civilians caught in the crossfire.

The Japanese Defenses: A Fortress of Death

Unlike previous battles, Japan did not try to defend the beaches.

Instead, they dug deep into Okinawa's hills, creating an impenetrable network of caves, tunnels, and bunkers.

General Mitsuru Ushijima, the Japanese commander, planned to drag the battle out as long as possible. 130,000 Japanese troops, including conscripted Okinawan civilians, were hidden across the island. Thousands of suicidal kamikaze pilots were prepared to attack U.S. ships.

Japan's strategy was simple: Make the Americans suffer so much that they would reconsider invading Japan.

The Battle Begins – A Deceptive Calm

The invasion of Okinawa began on April 1, 1945, with a massive amphibious assault by U.S. forces, under the command of Lieutenant General Simon Bolivar Buckner Jr., landing on the Hagushi beaches on the western coast of Okinawa.

American LCTs unload supplies on Yellow Beach

The initial landings were met with surprisingly light resistance from the Japanese defenders. The Japanese, under the command of Lieutenant General Mitsuru Ushijima, had opted for a defense in depth strategy, withdrawing their forces from the beaches and concentrating them in fortified positions further inland.

This deceptive calm allowed the Americans to quickly establish a beachhead and secure key positions on the island, including the strategically important Kadena and Yontan airfields. However, the initial lack of resistance was merely a tactical maneuver by the Japanese, who were preparing for a protracted and bloody defense of the island's southern region.

Japanese Defensive Strategy: A War of Attrition

The Japanese defensive strategy on Okinawa was based on the concept of attrition, aiming to inflict maximum casualties on the American forces and delay their advance towards the Japanese mainland. The Japanese, recognizing their inferiority in firepower and resources, sought to make the battle as costly as possible for the Americans, hoping to weaken their resolve and force them to negotiate a more favorable peace settlement.

The Japanese defenses were concentrated in the southern part of the island, where the terrain was more rugged and mountainous, providing natural defensive advantages. They had constructed a series of heavily fortified defensive lines, including the Shuri Line, which was anchored on a series of hills and ridges and protected by a network of bunkers, tunnels, and caves.

The Japanese also employed a variety of tactics to slow the American advance, including ambushes, sniper fire, and night attacks. They also made extensive use of mines and booby traps, which inflicted heavy casualties on the American forces.

Kamikaze Attacks: A Weapon of Despair

One of the most terrifying aspects of the Battle of Okinawa was the Japanese use of kamikaze attacks, with pilots deliberately crashing their planes into Allied ships, sacrificing their lives in the hope of inflicting maximum damage and demoralizing the enemy.

Over 1,500 kamikaze planes were sent against the U.S. fleet, attacking in waves of destruction. USS Bunker Hill, a U.S. aircraft carrier, was struck by two kamikaze planes within minutes, killing over 390 sailors and sending hundreds more into the sea.

For the U.S. Navy, Okinawa became a nightmare of fire, steel, and suicide bombers.

◻ *DID YOU KNOW*

- *The USS Laffey, a destroyer, was attacked by 22 kamikaze planes in a single day. Despite being hit multiple times, it miraculously survived - earning the nickname "The Ship That Would Not Die."*

- *The Japanese battleship Yamato, the largest and most powerful battleship ever built, was sent on a one-way mission to defend Okinawa. Without air cover, it was sunk by American bombers and torpedo planes before it could even reach the island.*

The Fight for Shuri Castle: The Bloodiest Land Battle of the Pacific

The most brutal phase of the battle came as U.S. forces tried to capture Shuri Castle, the heart of the Japanese defensive line.

The castle was surrounded by bunkers, caves, and machine-gun nests, making it nearly impossible to breach. For weeks, U.S. troops fought in brutal conditions - heavy rain turned the battlefield into a swamp of blood and mud. Japanese snipers and artillery turned every hill and valley into a killing zone. Thousands of U.S. troops were wounded or killed, and the battle dragged on for nearly two months.

It was the deadliest ground battle in the Pacific War.

Prolonged Fighting: A Grueling Struggle

The Battle of Okinawa was a protracted and grueling struggle, with intense close-quarters combat, heavy casualties, and widespread destruction.

The Americans, with their superior firepower and resources, gradually pushed their way southward, capturing key Japanese positions and inflicting heavy losses on the enemy. However, the Japanese, fighting from their well-prepared defenses and employing their attrition strategy, made the Americans pay a high price for every advance.

Two Marines from the 2nd Battalion, 1st Marine Regiment during fighting at Wana Ridge during the Battle of Okinawa, May 1945.

The battle raged for weeks, with both sides suffering heavy casualties. The Americans employed a combination of infantry assaults, artillery barrages, and air strikes to dislodge the Japanese from their positions, but the defenders fought tenaciously, often to the last man.

◻ **DID YOU KNOW**

- *Japanese defenders placed grenades inside the bodies of dead soldiers and civilians, turning them into deadly booby-traps for U.S. Marines searching the battlefield.*

- *Some U.S. military leaders, frustrated by Japan's stubborn resistance, proposed using poison gas on the island. However, President Truman and his advisors rejected the idea due to moral concerns and potential retaliation.*

Final Stages: The Fall of Okinawa

The final stages of the Battle of Okinawa were marked by increasing desperation on both sides. The Japanese, facing imminent defeat, launched a series of desperate counterattacks, hoping to inflict as many casualties as possible on the Americans.

A U.S. Marine Corps Grumman TBM Avenger dropping 227 kg bombs over Okinawa.

The Americans, determined to end the battle and secure the island, intensified their attacks, using their overwhelming firepower to push the Japanese back. The fighting was particularly intense in the southern part of the island, where the Japanese had concentrated their remaining forces.

On June 21, 1945, Lieutenant General Buckner, the commander of the U.S. Tenth Army, was killed by Japanese artillery fire, becoming the highest-ranking American officer killed in action during World War II.

The Final Days: Japan's Last Stand

By June 1945, the battle was nearly over, but the Japanese refused to surrender. General Ushijima ordered one final suicide attack, but by then, most of his men were either dead or too wounded to fight. On June 22, 1945, Ushijima and his officers committed ritual suicide, refusing to be captured. The remaining Japanese troops fought to the last bullet, and many killed themselves.

After 82 days of brutal combat, Okinawa was finally declared secure.

◻ **DID YOU KNOW**

- *The U.S. dropped millions of leaflets over Okinawa, urging the Japanese soldiers and civilians to surrender. The U.S. also wanted to undermine Japanese propaganda, which told troops and civilians that Americans would torture and kill prisoners. Leaflets gave clear instructions on how to surrender safely.*

The rear gunner of a Douglas A-26 of the 319th Bomb Group is ready to drop leaflets on Okinawa.

Okinawa proved to be the costliest battle of the Pacific War. The U.S. lost 12,500 U.S. soldiers, sailors, and Marines, with more than 50,000 wounded - the highest number of U.S. casualties in the Pacific.

More than 100,000 Japanese soldiers killed. Only 7,000 Japanese soldiers surrendered - the rest fought to the death.

Civilian Tragedy on Okinawa

The greatest horror of Okinawa was not just the battle itself - but the massive loss of civilian life. More than 100,000 Okinawan civilians were killed. Many were caught in the crossfire, while others were forced to fight by the Japanese military. Some committed suicide rather than surrender, fearing the Americans after years of propaganda. Entire families jumped off cliffs to their deaths, believing they had no other choice.

Okinawa became one of the greatest civilian tragedies of World War II.

Shaping History - The Battle That Shaped the Atomic Bomb Decision

The sheer brutality of Okinawa convinced U.S. leaders that invading Japan would be catastrophic. If Japan fought this hard for one island, what would happen on the mainland?

Estimates predicted that an invasion of Japan would cost over 1 million American lives and millions of Japanese deaths. This played a major role in President Harry Truman's decision to use atomic bombs on Hiroshima and Nagasaki.

For those who survived, Okinawa was a nightmare that never ended.

For the world, it was a warning of the true cost of war.

And for history, it was the last great battle before peace would finally arrive.

CHAPTER 16: THE RACE TO JAPAN AND THE ATMOIC BOMBS – THE ENDGAME (1945)

By 1945, the Allied forces in the Pacific had pushed the Japanese back to their home islands, poised for a final showdown that promised to be a bloody and protracted struggle. The island-hopping campaign, while successful in capturing key strategic positions, had also exposed the fierce resistance and determination of the Japanese defenders. As the Allies prepared for the invasion of Japan, they faced a daunting challenge, one that threatened to inflict unprecedented casualties and prolong the war indefinitely.

On April 12, 1945, President Franklin D. Roosevelt died, being replaced by Harry S Truman. Some Japanese leaders believed it might lead to a change in U.S. policy, possibly opening the door for negotiations or a more favorable peace settlement.

However, as news of Roosevelt's death spread, it became clear that the U.S. was not likely to change its strategy. Japanese leaders, particularly militarists, continued to push for a fight to the bitter end, believing they could still negotiate a better outcome.

The "Ketsu-Go" Strategy: A Nation Mobilized for War

The Japanese government adopted a policy of "Ketsu-Go," or decisive battle, which called for a final, all-out defense of the homeland. The Ketsu-Go strategy was based on the belief that by inflicting heavy casualties on the Allies, Japan could force them to negotiate a more favorable peace settlement that would preserve its sovereignty and its imperial system.

The Ketsu-Go strategy involved the mobilization of the entire nation for war. Civilians, including women and children, were trained to fight with bamboo spears and other makeshift weapons. The government also launched a massive propaganda campaign, exhorting the population to resist the Allied invasion and fight to the death for the emperor and the nation.

Bushido, the "way of the warrior," was a code of conduct and ethical principles that guided the samurai class in feudal Japan. It emphasized loyalty, honor, courage, self-sacrifice, and a disdain for death. These values were revived and promoted by the government and military to inspire the population and galvanize them for a total war effort. Its emphasis on honor and self-sacrifice was used to encourage Japanese soldiers and civilians to fight to the death rather than surrender, which was seen as a betrayal of the emperor and the nation.

The Dilemma: Invasion or Alternative?

The mounting casualties in the Pacific War raised serious concerns among American military and political leaders, and presented a dilemma. The prospect of invading the Japanese home islands, where the Japanese were expected to fight even more fanatically, was daunting. Estimates of potential American casualties in an invasion of Japan ranged from hundreds of thousands to over a million.

The development of the atomic bomb, a weapon of unprecedented destructive power, offered a potential alternative to a costly invasion. The atomic bomb's potential to end the war quickly and avoid a protracted and bloody invasion was undeniable, but its use was also fraught with moral and ethical dilemmas.

The decision to use the atomic bomb was a complex and controversial one, with arguments for and against its use. Ultimately, the decision was made to drop atomic bombs on the Japanese cities of Hiroshima and Nagasaki in August 1945, leading to Japan's surrender and the end of World War II.

The Tokyo Firebombing (March 9-10, 1945): The Deadliest Air Raid

Before deploying the atom bomb, to break Japan's will, the U.S. turned to a new strategy: the systematic destruction of its cities. Initially, the U.S. had tried precision bombing, targeting factories and military installations.

But there was a problem. High-altitude bombing was inaccurate, especially over cities covered in smoke or clouds. Japan's industry was spread out - many factories were small workshops in civilian neighborhoods, and most of Japan's cities were made of wood, making them extremely vulnerable to fire.

One of the most devastating raids of the bombing campaign was the firebombing of Tokyo on March 9-10, 1945. The raid, codenamed Operation Meetinghouse, involved over 300 B-29 bombers, flying at just 5,000 to 9,000 feet to ensure maximum accuracy, dropping 1,700 tons of incendiary bombs on the Japanese capital, creating a firestorm that engulfed a large portion of the city.

Tokyo burns under B-29 firebomb assault.

The attack lasted 6 hours and was horrific, resulting in an estimated 100,000 deaths and the destruction of over 267,000 buildings. 1 million people were left homeless, and a quarter of Tokyo was destroyed. The firestorm created by the incendiary bombs was so intense that it generated winds that sucked people into the flames and melted asphalt roads.

The Destruction of Japan's Other Cities

The success of the Tokyo firebombing led to a relentless campaign against Japan's urban centers.

Osaka (March 13-14, 1945)

B-29 bombers destroyed one-third of the city, killing over 10,000 people.

Nagoya (March 19, 1945)

The industrial center of Japan, home to aircraft and arms factories, was bombed repeatedly. Almost half the city was destroyed.

Kobe (June 5, 1945)

Another major industrial city was nearly wiped off the map.

Yokohama (May 29, 1945)

10,000 civilians were killed overnight, and the city was left in ruins.

By mid-1945, over 60 Japanese cities had been bombed, killing hundreds of thousands and leaving millions homeless.

▫ *DID YOU KNOW*

- *Over 330,000 civilians died in firebombing raids across Japan - more civilians than both atomic bombs combined.*

Despite the bombing campaign, and the destruction inflicted, Japan still did not surrender. It convinced the U.S. government that even complete destruction of cities might not force Japan's surrender. The atomic bomb was seen as the final, ultimate weapon to end the war.

The legacy of the bombing campaign remains a subject of debate, with some historians arguing that it was a necessary evil to force Japan's surrender and avoid a costly invasion of the home islands. Others argue that the bombing campaign was morally reprehensible, causing unnecessary suffering and destruction.

The Manhattan Project: Creating the Bomb

The decision to use atomic bombs on Hiroshima and Nagasaki in August 1945 remains one of the most controversial and debated events in human history. It was a decision that brought a swift end to World War II, but it also ushered in the nuclear age, a new era fraught with the potential for unimaginable destruction.

The atomic bomb was the result of the top-secret Manhattan Project, a multi-year effort involving thousands of scientists, engineers, and military personnel.

The Origins of the Bomb

The idea of atomic weapons began in 1939, when scientists Albert Einstein and Leo Szilard warned the U.S. that Nazi Germany might be developing nuclear weapons.

In response, the U.S. launched the Manhattan Project in 1942, with research centers in Los Alamos, New Mexico; Oak Ridge, Tennessee; and Hanford, Washington. The first successful test of an atomic bomb—the Trinity Test—took place on July 16, 1945, in the New Mexico desert.

J. Robert Oppenheimer, an American theoretical physicist who served as the director of the Manhattan Project's Los Alamos Laboratory during World War II.

The Two Types of Bombs

The U.S. developed two atomic bombs, each with a different design:

- **"Little Boy" (Hiroshima)** – A uranium-based bomb.

- **"Fat Man" (Nagasaki)** – A more powerful plutonium-based bomb.

Both bombs were ready by late July 1945 - just as the war was reaching its climax.

Fat Man bomb being placed on trailer cradle in front of Assembly Building.

The Debate: Bomb or Invasion?

Before deciding to drop the atomic bombs, U.S. leaders debated alternative ways to end the war.

Option 1: Invade Japan (Operation Downfall)

The U.S. planned to launch a full-scale invasion of Japan in late 1945. Military experts estimated 1 million U.S. troops would die, and up to 10 million Japanese civilians and soldiers would perish.

The battles for Iwo Jima and Okinawa had shown Japan's willingness to fight to the last man. Japan planned to mobilize civilians, including women and children, for a final defense.

Option 2: Demonstrate the Bomb in a Non-Populated Area

Some scientists suggested dropping the bomb on an uninhabited island to scare Japan into surrendering. However, U.S. officials feared Japan might ignore the demonstration, and if the bomb failed to detonate, the U.S. would look weak.

Option 3: Wait for the Soviet Union to Attack Japan

On July 26, 1945, the Allies issued the Potsdam Declaration, demanding Japan's unconditional surrender. At the same time, the Soviet Union was preparing to invade Japan from the north. Some U.S. officials believed that Soviet intervention could force Japan's surrender without the atomic bomb.

The Final Decision: Drop the Bomb

After weighing the options, Truman decided to use the atomic bomb. His reasoning was simple:

"A quarter of a million of our young men were preparing to die in a land invasion. I was convinced that the bomb would save more lives in the long run."

On July 25, 1945, Truman gave the order:

"Release the bomb as soon as possible after August 3, depending on weather."

The countdown to Hiroshima had begun.

The Atomic Bombings: The Day the World Changed

The selection of targets for the atomic bombs was entrusted to a Target Committee, a group of military and scientific experts convened in May 1945, led by Manhattan Project scientist Dr. William Penney.

Hiroshima, on the southern coast of Honshu Island, was chosen as it was a major military hub with large depots, troop concentrations, and the headquarters of Japan's Second Army, responsible for the defense of southern Japan. The city was a vital supply and logistics hub with factories and facilities supporting Japan's war effort. Hiroshima's relatively flat terrain and dense urban layout made it ideal for assessing the bomb's destructive capacity. The nearby mountains would contain and amplify the blast effects.

Nagasaki, a port city located on the western coast of Kyushu Island, was a key industrial city with factories producing war materials such as ships, torpedoes, and steel. Nagasaki was not the primary target for August 9; the bomb was initially intended for Kokura, another industrial city. However, poor weather and heavy cloud cover over Kokura forced the mission to redirect to Nagasaki.

◻ **DID YOU KNOW**

- *The original primary target was Kyoto, but U.S. Secretary of War Henry Stimson personally removed it from the list because he had visited the city and admired its cultural heritage. Hiroshima was chosen instead.*

Hiroshima – A City Obliterated August 6, 1945

At 8:15 AM, the atomic bomb, nicknamed "Little Boy," exploded 1,900 feet above Hiroshima, unleashing the power of 15,000 tons of TNT.

80,000 people died instantly—men, women, and children.

Hiroshima, 1945.

The blast wave flattened everything within a two-mile radius. The heat flash ignited thousands of fires, creating a firestorm that engulfed the city. Metal melted, bricks turned to ash, and people were incinerated where they stood. Over 60,000 more would die in the following months from burns, radiation sickness, and injuries. The city's hospitals were destroyed, leaving survivors with no medical help.

One survivor, Akiko Takahashi, later recalled:

"I turned to my friend, and in that instant, she was gone. Just... gone. I could see her shadow on the wall, but she was no longer there."

The explosion sucked oxygen from the air, creating winds stronger than a hurricane. Fire spread rapidly, engulfing homes, factories, and temples. Survivors who weren't killed by the blast were trapped in the flames.

One witness described the horror:

"The rivers filled with the burned bodies of those who had jumped in to escape the flames. The water boiled. The air smelled of death."

But Japan did not surrender.

Nagasaki – A Second Apocalypse August 9, 1945

With no surrender forthcoming, just 3 days later on August 9, a second atomic bomb - "Fat Man" - was dropped on Nagasaki, a city of 263,000 people.

At 11:02 AM, the bomb detonated over the Urakami district, home to schools, factories, and a historic cathedral. The blast was even more powerful than Hiroshima, with the force of 21,000 tons of TNT.

Mushroom cloud above Nagasaki after atomic bombing on August 9, 1945.

40,000 people died instantly, and another 40,000 perished within weeks. Survivors suffered from horrific burns and deadly radiation poisoning. Entire districts vanished in seconds.

One survivor, Dr. Nagai Takashi, described the moment:

"A white light filled my hospital room, and I was thrown to the ground. When I stood up, the city I knew was gone. Only fire remained."

For those who survived, the days after the bombings were a nightmare beyond imagination.

Survivors, known as hibakusha, wandered the ruins, their skin hanging in strips, their hair burned away. Many were blinded by the flash or suffered internal bleeding from radiation. The smell of burned flesh and smoke filled the air for weeks.

A young girl named Sadako Sasaki, just two years old during the blast, later developed leukemia from radiation exposure. She spent her final days folding paper cranes, hoping for a miracle.

The Unseen Killer: Radiation Sickness

Within days, survivors began falling ill with mysterious symptoms—vomiting, fever, and hair loss. Radiation poisoning destroyed their bodies from the inside out. Many who appeared healthy after the bombings died weeks or months later.

A doctor treating the wounded wrote in his journal:

> *"We didn't understand. The patients who seemed fine yesterday were dead today. There was nothing we could do."*

The Total Destruction of Two Cities

By the end of 1945, over 200,000 people had died from the two bombings.

Hiroshima and Nagasaki were reduced to rubble. More than 70% of all buildings were destroyed. Survivors lived in the ruins, suffering from hunger, disease, and radiation exposure.

This time, Japan's leaders could no longer deny reality.

▫ DID YOU KNOW

- *The U.S. had a third atomic bomb ready by mid-August and planned to drop it on August 19, 1945, if Japan did not surrender. Additional bombs were being prepared for continued use.*

Japan's Surrender: The End of World War II

On August 15, 1945, Emperor Hirohito announced Japan's surrender, marking the end of World War II.

> *"The war situation has developed not necessarily to Japan's advantage...we have to endure the unendurable and bear the unbearable"*

For the first time in history, Japan's people heard their Emperor's voice on the radio. In his speech, Hirohito did not use the word "surrender." Instead, he used carefully chosen words to protect Japan's dignity.

Some Japanese wept in relief. Others collapsed in despair. Some fell to their knees in shock, unable to comprehend that the Empire of Japan - once thought invincible - had surrendered.

It was a moment that changed the world forever.

World War II was finally over.

The Day the World Changed Forever

The bombings of Hiroshima and Nagasaki were the most devastating single attacks in human history. The bombs ended World War II, and saved lives, but left scars that would never heal. They also changed warfare forever, making the world fear nuclear destruction.

Even today, the shadows of Hiroshima and Nagasaki remain - reminders of what happens when war reaches its absolute extreme.

And a warning that it must never happen again.

Hibakusha: The Voices of the Survivors

The survivors of Hiroshima and Nagasaki, known as hibakusha, spent their lives telling their stories, warning the world about the horrors of nuclear war.

The Hiroshima Peace Memorial

In 1955, the city of Hiroshima built the Peace Memorial Park, including the ruins of the Atomic Dome. Each year, on August 6, Japan holds a moment of silence for the victims.

The Call for Nuclear Disarmament

Survivors have dedicated their lives to advocating for peace. Japan remains one of the world's strongest voices against nuclear weapons.

One survivor, Setsuko Thurlow, later spoke at the United Nations:

> *"We must never allow another Hiroshima. Never allow another Nagasaki. No human being should ever suffer what we suffered."*

The World Reacts: The End of World War II

When news of Japan's surrender reached the United States, Britain, and other Allied nations, people erupted in celebration. In New York City, crowds flooded Times Square, cheering and waving flags. In London, church bells rang, and fireworks lit up the sky. In San Francisco, a sailor famously kissed a nurse in the streets, captured in one of the most iconic photos in history.

After six years of global warfare, the deadliest conflict in human history was finally over.

Although Japan had announced its surrender on August 15, the formal signing took place on September 2, 1945, aboard the USS Missouri in Tokyo Bay.

Japanese representatives, dressed in black suits, signed the official surrender documents.

Japanese Foreign Minister Mamoru Shigemitsu signs the Instrument of Surrender on behalf of the Japanese Government, on board USS Missouri, 2 September 1945. Lieutenant General Richard K. Sutherland, U.S. Army.

General Douglas MacArthur, the Supreme Allied Commander, declared:

"Today, the guns are silent. The skies no longer rain death. A great tragedy has ended."

With the stroke of a pen, World War II was officially over.

CHAPTER 17: WHY JAPAN'S STRATEGY FAILED

Japan entered World War II with bold ambitions but an overextended strategy that ultimately led to its defeat. Initial successes masked deep flaws - overconfidence, inadequate resources, and underestimation of the industrial power of the U.S. Strategic miscalculations drained Japan's strength. Let's take a look at the critical weaknesses in Japan's war strategy and how they led to its downfall.

Fighting on Too Many Fronts

Japan's vast ambitions in World War II led to a fatal flaw: overextension. Fighting simultaneously in China, the Pacific, and Southeast Asia stretched its military, and resources too thin, making it unable to sustain a prolonged war against the Allies. The failure to prioritize and consolidate resources proved disastrous, serving as a cautionary lesson in military strategy.

The China Quagmire

Japan's invasion of China in 1937 became a costly, drawn-out conflict, tying down over a million troops. This prolonged war drained resources and diverted attention from the looming Pacific conflict.

The Pacific Theater: A Two-Front War

The attack on Pearl Harbor in 1941 brought the U.S. into the war, forcing Japan to fight across the vast Pacific. Despite early victories, Japan's forces were gradually overwhelmed by America's industrial and military superiority. The island-hopping campaign, battles at Midway and Guadalcanal, and relentless naval warfare eroded Japan's strength.

Southeast Asia: A Logistical Burden

Japan's conquest of Southeast Asia secured vital resources but opened another vulnerable front. Defending these territories against Allied counterattacks and guerrilla resistance stretched its military even further.

Consequences of Overextension

Juggling multiple fronts weakened Japan's ability to concentrate its forces. The prolonged war in China, relentless U.S. advances in the Pacific, and the defensive burden in Southeast Asia left Japan overcommitted and unable to counter Allied offensives effectively.

Economic and Industrial Limitations

Japan's war strategy was crippled by a fundamental weakness: limited economic and industrial capacity. It could not compete with the massive industrial power of the United States, leading to its eventual defeat. The war exposed the critical role of economic strength in military success, showing how a nation's ability to sustain its war machine can determine the outcome of a conflict.

Resource Dependence: A Fatal Vulnerability

Japan lacked essential resources like oil, iron, and rubber, relying heavily on imports. The Allied naval blockade cut off these supplies, strangling Japan's war production and crippling its military operations.

Industrial Disparity: Outmatched by the U.S.

Japan's industrial output was dwarfed by the U.S., which could mass-produce ships, planes, and weapons at an overwhelming rate. American technological innovations, like radar and sonar, further widened the gap.

The Oil Embargo: A Devastating Blow

The U.S. oil embargo of 1941 cut off 80% of Japan's oil supply, forcing rationing and fueling desperation. This shortage severely weakened Japan's military and played a key role in its decision to go to war with the U.S.

A War Japan Couldn't Sustain

Japan's inability to match Allied production or secure resources led to its downfall. It was outproduced, outgunned, and outlasted, with no way to sustain its war effort against an increasingly powerful enemy.

Strategic Missteps

Japan's flawed strategy - misjudging the U.S., overextending its forces, and miscalculating the war's duration - sealed its fate. The war highlighted the dangers of strategic overreach and underestimating an opponent's resolve and capabilities.

The Pearl Harbor Gamble: A Costly Miscalculation

The attack on Pearl Harbor, meant to cripple the U.S. Pacific Fleet and deter American intervention, backfired. Instead of forcing the U.S. into submission, it galvanized American resolve, ensuring a determined and well-resourced enemy.

Overextension: An Empire Spread Too Thin

Japan's rapid expansion overstretched its forces across a vast territory, straining logistics and defenses. The Allies exploited this by using an island-hopping strategy, bypassing strongholds and cutting off Japan's supply lines.

Underestimating the Allies: A Fatal Error

Japanese leaders wrongly assumed the U.S. would be unwilling or unable to sustain a long war. They underestimated America's industrial capacity and military buildup, which ultimately overwhelmed Japan.

A War Japan Couldn't Win

These strategic failures left Japan vulnerable to Allied offensives. Overconfidence led to poor planning, and misjudging the U.S. resulted in a prolonged war Japan lacked the resources to sustain.

Technological and Tactical Disadvantages

Japan's failure to keep pace with technological innovations and its reliance on outdated, unsustainable tactics played a major role in its downfall. The war highlighted the necessity of adaptability and innovation in modern warfare.

Lagging in Radar and Codebreaking

The Allies, particularly the U.S. and Britain, developed advanced radar systems and codebreaking capabilities that gave them a crucial edge. Japan's inferior radar limited its ability to detect enemy movements, while its weak codebreaking efforts left it blind to Allied plans - leading to devastating losses, such as at Midway.

Unsustainable Tactics

Japan's reliance on aggressive but costly tactics, such as banzai charges and kamikaze attacks, inflicted damage but also led to high casualties and depleted its experienced forces. While these strategies reflected Japan's warrior ethos, they proved ineffective against the Allies' superior firepower and resources.

Consequences and Collapse

Japan's technological inferiority and wasteful tactics gradually weakened its military effectiveness. Its inability to counter Allied advancements in intelligence and warfare contributed to mounting defeats, draining its manpower and resources.

Loss of Naval and Air Superiority

Japan's early success relied on its powerful navy and air force, but this dominance was short-lived. A series of key defeats and the relentless U.S. island-hopping campaign gradually eroded Japan's ability to wage war effectively.

Midway: The Turning Point

The Battle of Midway (June 1942) was a decisive blow to Japan's naval power. The U.S., leveraging intelligence and superior tactics, sank four Japanese carriers and killed many experienced pilots. This defeat marked the beginning of Japan's decline, shifting the war's momentum to the Allies.

The Decline of the Imperial Navy

After Midway, the U.S. outproduced Japan in ships and aircraft, while battles like Guadalcanal and Leyte Gulf (1944) inflicted massive losses. By war's end, the Imperial Japanese Navy (IJN) was effectively destroyed, unable to mount major operations or protect supply lines.

The Erosion of Air Power

Japan's air force suffered from pilot attrition and outdated aircraft. While the U.S. developed superior planes like the F6F Hellcat, Japan struggled to replace its lost Zero fighters. Strategic bombing campaigns, especially from B-29 Superfortresses, further crippled Japan's war industry.

The Consequences

Losing naval and air superiority left Japan defenseless, unable to project power or resist Allied advances. The psychological impact was profound, replacing early confidence with despair as the U.S. closed in on the home islands.

Internal Political and Social Issues

Rigid leadership, the emperor's passivity, and a crumbling home front eroded Japan's ability to sustain the war. Unable to adapt to Allied advances, Japan's internal weaknesses proved as damaging as battlefield defeats.

Rigid Military Leadership

Japan's military leadership prioritized hierarchy and tradition over adaptability. Consensus-driven decision-making slowed responses, while dissent was discouraged, stifling strategic innovation. This rigidity became a liability as the war turned against Japan.

The Emperor's Silence

Emperor Hirohito, though revered, largely deferred to military leaders. His reluctance to challenge aggressive policies reinforced a culture of conformity, limiting Japan's ability to reassess its failing strategy.

Declining Morale on the Home Front

Allied blockades and bombing campaigns devastated Japan's economy, causing shortages and widespread suffering. As losses mounted, public morale declined, weakening war production, civilian mobilization, and government authority.

Allied Technological Superiority

Among the many factors that led to Japan's defeat, Allied technological superiority - culminating in the atomic bomb - was decisive. This unprecedented weapon forced Japan's surrender and reshaped modern warfare.

The Manhattan Project: A Secret Race

The Manhattan Project, launched in 1939, brought together top scientists, including Einstein, Oppenheimer, and Fermi, in a race to develop an atomic bomb before Nazi Germany. Working in secrecy, researchers at Los Alamos successfully tested the first bomb on July 16, 1945.

Unleashing Atomic Power

The bomb's immense power came from nuclear fission, which released massive energy by splitting atomic nuclei. The first bomb, "Little Boy," was dropped on Hiroshima on August 6, 1945; the second, "Fat Man," devastated Nagasaki on August 9.

Unprecedented Destruction

The bombings killed tens of thousands instantly and left cities in ruins. Radiation exposure caused long-term health effects, leaving a lasting impact on survivors and generations to come. The psychological shock of such destruction also weighed heavily on Japan.

A Controversial Decision

Debate continues over whether the bombings were necessary. Some argue they prevented a costly invasion and saved lives; others see them as an unnecessary tragedy that introduced the threat of nuclear annihilation.

Japan's Surrender

Combined with the Soviet Union's declaration of war on August 8, the bombings forced Japan's unconditional surrender on August 15, 1945, ending World War II. The world entered a new era - one of nuclear power and global uncertainty.

CHAPTER 19: HEROES OF THE PACIFIC WAR

The Pacific War was a crucible of courage, where ordinary individuals rose to extraordinary heights of bravery and selflessness. While many heroes were recognized and celebrated, countless others performed extraordinary deeds that went largely unnoticed or were only acknowledged posthumously. Let's delve into the stories of just some of these unsung heroes, their remarkable acts of valor, and their unwavering commitment to their comrades.

U.S. Marine Corporal Charles W. Lindberg – Flag Raising on Iwo Jima

Lindberg was part of the group that raised the first U.S. flag on Mount Suribachi during the Battle of Iwo Jima (February 1945).

Though overshadowed by the iconic second flag-raising photograph, his bravery during the intense fighting, and relentless Japanese resistance, epitomized the perseverance of Marines on Iwo Jima.

The flag raising was a moment that captured the spirit of courage and determination that defined the American fighting spirit in the Pacific.

Private Desmond T. Doss - The Hero of Hacksaw Ridge, Okinawa

A devout Seventh-day Adventist and conscientious objector, Doss served as a medic in the Battle of Okinawa, refusing to carry a weapon due to his faith. Despite ridicule from fellow soldiers, he proved his courage on Hacksaw Ridge, a heavily defended escarpment.

Desmond Doss

The ridge was heavily defended by Japanese troops, and the fighting was particularly intense and brutal. Doss, unarmed and undeterred, repeatedly braved enemy fire to rescue his wounded comrades. He lowered them one by one down the steep cliffs of Hacksaw Ridge, using a rope and a litter, under constant enemy fire.

Doss's actions were nothing short of miraculous. He saved the lives of an estimated 75 soldiers, without firing a single shot. He was awarded the Medal of Honor, the highest military decoration for valor, for his "outstanding bravery and unflinching determination in the face of desperately dangerous conditions."

U.S. Navy Chief Petty Officer Doris Miller - Hero of Pearl Harbor

Amidst the chaos and destruction of the attack on Pearl Harbour, a young African American sailor named Doris Miller displayed remarkable bravery. Amidst the chaos and destruction, and with no training, he manned an anti-aircraft gun and helped rescue wounded sailors.

Admiral Chester W. Nimitz pins the Navy Cross on Doris Miller, Pearl Harbor, May 27, 1942

For his heroism, Miller became the first African American to receive the Navy Cross, a groundbreaking moment that challenged racial barriers in the U.S. Navy and paved the way for greater opportunities for Black service members.

British Indian Army Sepoy Kamal Ram - Victoria Cross Hero of Burma

Sepoy Kamal Ram of the British Indian Army displayed extraordinary bravery in the Burma Campaign, earning the Victoria Cross—the highest military decoration for gallantry in the British Commonwealth.

King George VI pinning the Victoria Cross on Sepoy Kamal Ram, 26 July 1944.

Born in 1924 in Punjab, British India, Ram enlisted at 17 and served in the 8th Battalion, 19th Hyderabad Regiment. During the Battle of Bishenpur in May 1944, his unit was pinned down by heavy Japanese fire. With his commander killed and the advance stalled, Ram volunteered to attack a heavily fortified bunker. Crawling under intense fire, he single-handedly eliminated the defenders, securing a crucial victory.

For his exceptional valor, Ram became the first Indian soldier awarded the Victoria Cross in World War II, symbolizing the courage and sacrifice of Indian troops in the Burma Campaign.

Private First Class Eugene B. Sledge - A Marine's Story of Survival and Sacrifice

Eugene B. Sledge, a Marine mortarman, fought in some of the Pacific War's most brutal battles, from Peleliu to Okinawa. His memoir, With the Old Breed, captures the harrowing reality of combat and the resilience of the soldiers who endured it.

Born in 1923 in Mobile, Alabama, Sledge enlisted in the U.S. Marine Corps in 1942. Assigned to the 1st Marine Division, he experienced the carnage of Peleliu in 1944, witnessing the horrors of war and the unbreakable camaraderie among Marines. He later fought in Okinawa, enduring even greater devastation.

After the war, Sledge became a professor and chronicled his experiences in With the Old Breed, now a classic of war literature. His memoir provides an unflinching account of battle's brutality while reflecting on the lasting psychological toll of war.

U.S. Army Technician Fifth Grade John R. Towle - Hero of the Leyte Campaign

Serving with the 32nd Infantry Division in the Philippines, Towle balanced dual roles as a radio operator and medic, maintaining communication while risking his life to aid wounded comrades.

Towle repeatedly demonstrated his courage and compassion by risking his life to rescue injured soldiers. He would often venture into active combat zones, unarmed and exposed to enemy fire, to reach wounded comrades and provide them with medical aid.

During the Battle of Limon, he braved enemy fire to rescue a wounded soldier stranded in open terrain, administering aid and carrying him to safety under relentless Japanese gunfire. His selfless bravery earned him the Silver Star for gallantry in action.

The Chindits - Guerrilla Warfare in Burma

The Chindits were elite, long-range raiders who operated deep behind Japanese lines in Burma, disrupting supply routes, gathering intelligence, and tying down enemy forces.

The Chindits were the brainchild of Major General Orde Wingate, a charismatic and unconventional British officer with a passion for guerrilla warfare. Wingate, a veteran of the campaigns in Palestine and Ethiopia, believed that small, highly trained units could operate effectively behind enemy lines, disrupting their operations and tying down their forces.

The Chindits were recruited from volunteers from various British and Commonwealth units, including the British Army, the Indian Army, and the Gurkha regiments. The selection process was rigorous, as the Chindits needed to be physically fit, mentally tough, and highly skilled in jungle warfare.

Chindits preparing a meal beside a temple on Ramree Island, Burma, January 1945.

They underwent intensive training, learning to navigate the jungle, operate in small units, and conduct long-range patrols. They were also trained in demolitions, communications, and medical skills, as they would be operating deep behind enemy lines with limited support.

Their first mission, Operation Longcloth (1943), saw 3,000 men penetrate Japanese territory. The Chindits marched for weeks through dense jungle, carrying their own supplies and equipment. They faced numerous challenges, including disease, starvation, and the constant threat of ambush by Japanese patrols. Despite these hardships, the Chindits achieved significant successes. They disrupted Japanese supply lines, destroyed bridges and communication lines, gathered valuable intelligence, and proved the effectiveness of jungle warfare tactics

In Operation Thursday (1944), a larger force of 9,000—airlifted into enemy territory—established fortified bases and aided the main Allied offensive. The Japanese, now aware of the Chindit threat, were better prepared to counter their operations. The monsoon season also hampered the Chindits' movements and made it difficult to maintain supply lines.

Despite these challenges, the Chindits achieved significant successes, and played a key role in the Burma Campaign, notably contributing to the victory at Kohima.

U.S. Army Rangers - The Cabanatuan Raid: A Daring POW Rescue

In January 1945, U.S. Army Rangers and Filipino guerrillas launched a daring mission to rescue over 500 Allied POWs from a Japanese camp deep in enemy territory. Fearing the prisoners would be executed as Japan faced defeat, Lieutenant Colonel Henry Mucci and Captain Robert Prince devised a bold plan relying on stealth, surprise, and local support.

On January 30, the Rangers infiltrated the camp under cover of darkness, swiftly eliminating guards while guerrillas created diversions. Despite challenges, they liberated the POWs and began a perilous escape through enemy lines, aided by guerrillas.

The journey was arduous, with the POWs, weakened by years of captivity, struggling to keep up with the Rangers. However, the Rangers, inspired by their mission and their compassion for the POWs, carried the sick and injured, shared their rations, and provided encouragement.

After days of exhausting travel, they reached American forces, completing one of the most successful rescue missions of the war and proving the Allies' unwavering commitment to their own.

Lieutenant Commander Ernest E. Evans - Defiance at Leyte Gulf

In the epic Battle of Leyte Gulf, the USS Johnston, commanded by Lt. Cmdr. Ernest E. Evans, charged into overwhelming odds to protect American forces. Part of the outgunned "Taffy 3" task unit, Johnston faced a massive Japanese fleet of battleships and cruisers off Samar.

Lieutenant Commander Ernest E. Evans.

Despite being heavily outmatched, Evans ordered an aggressive attack, launching torpedoes and relentlessly firing at the enemy to disrupt their advance. Despite the overwhelming odds, Evans and his crew continued to fight, refusing to surrender. The Johnston, battered and crippled, eventually sank beneath the waves, taking with it Evans and many of his crew.

Evans was posthumously awarded the Medal of Honor for his extraordinary bravery and sacrifice.

Evans's last words, reportedly shouted to his crew as the ship went down, were "This is going to be a fight against overwhelming odds from which survival cannot be expected. We will do what damage we can."

Sergeant Major Jacob Vouza - The Indomitable Scout of Guadalcanal

Sergeant Major Jacob Vouza, a native scout from the Solomon Islands, was instrumental in the Guadalcanal Campaign. His deep knowledge of the terrain and unwavering loyalty to the Allies made him invaluable to the U.S. Marines.

In September 1942, Vouza was captured by the Japanese and brutally tortured in an attempt to extract Allied intelligence. Despite severe beatings and bayonet wounds, he refused to talk. Managing to escape, he crawled miles through the jungle.

Sergeant Major Jacob Charles Vouza, after WW2.

Upon reaching the American lines, Vouza, despite his wounds, insisted on delivering crucial intelligence about Japanese troop movements and positions. His information proved invaluable to the Marines, who were able to use it to their advantage in the upcoming battles.

Vouza's heroism was recognized by the Allied forces. He was awarded the Silver Star, the third-highest military decoration for valor in the U.S. Armed Forces, for his "gallantry in action."

Lieutenant John F. Kennedy and PT-109: A Test of Leadership

During World War II, the Solomon Islands became a battleground where young naval officer John F. Kennedy faced a harrowing test of courage. On the night of August 2, 1943, his patrol torpedo boat, PT-109, was rammed and sunk by a Japanese destroyer, leaving Kennedy and his crew stranded in enemy waters.

Despite his chronic back pain, Kennedy led his men to safety, towing an injured crew member for miles through treacherous waters. Over the next days, he swam between islands seeking help until two Solomon Islanders, Biuku Gasa and Eroni Kumana, helped alert Allied forces, leading to their rescue. Kennedy's resilience and leadership in this crisis foreshadowed his future presidency.

Filipino Guerrillas: The Resistance Against Japanese Occupation

After Japan occupied the Philippines in 1942, a determined guerrilla movement emerged, composed of ordinary Filipinos who refused to submit to foreign rule. Farmers, students, and teachers took up arms, using guerrilla tactics to harass Japanese forces, sabotage infrastructure, and gather intelligence for the Allies.

Their resistance disrupted Japanese control, tying down enemy troops and undermining supply lines. As the Allies launched their counteroffensive, the guerrillas played a crucial role—guiding troops, rescuing POWs, and conducting sabotage operations.

The fight came at a high cost. Many guerrillas were captured, tortured, or executed, while civilians faced brutal reprisals. Despite these hardships, their sacrifices helped pave the way for the liberation of the Philippines, proving vital to the Allied victory.

Nurses and Medics - Unsung Heroes of the Pacific War

Amidst the carnage of the Pacific War, nurses and medics displayed extraordinary courage and compassion, risking their lives to treat the wounded under relentless fire, disease, and exhaustion. Often referred to as "angels of mercy," they worked in field hospitals, on hospital ships, and even near the front lines, tending to soldiers with limited resources and amidst constant danger. Their duties were not only physically demanding but also emotionally draining. They witnessed firsthand the horrors of war, the devastating injuries, and the loss of life. Yet, they persevered, driven by a deep sense of duty and a profound compassion for their fellow human beings.

Nurses and medics were not immune to the dangers of combat. They often served in close proximity to the front lines, exposed to enemy fire, shelling, and air raids. Many were wounded or killed in action. Lieutenant Ann Bernatitus, a Navy nurse, braved enemy fire at Iwo Jima, earning the Bronze Star for her selfless service. Beyond treating battle injuries, these medical personnel waged war against malaria, dysentery, and other tropical diseases, often deadlier than combat itself.

Their dedication not only saved lives but also sustained the morale of the troops, leaving behind a legacy of sacrifice and compassion that remains an integral part of the war's history.

CHAPTER 19: WAR CRIMES AND THE COST OF WAR

After the war, attention turned to Japan's brutal treatment of POWs, which included torture, forced labor, and executions. Viewing surrender as dishonorable, Japanese soldiers saw captured enemies as weak and unworthy of respect. This belief dehumanized POWs, justifying, in Japanese minds, their harsh mistreatment. Let's look at some of this awful mistreatment.

The Bataan Death March (April 1942): A Journey of Suffering

After the fall of Bataan in the Philippines, 76,000 American and Filipino troops were forced to march 65 miles in brutal heat with little food or water. Thousands died from exhaustion, disease, beatings, and executions.

Japanese guards bayoneted or shot prisoners who collapsed. Some guards took pleasure in torturing the prisoners, forcing them to stand in the sun for hours or making them drink filthy, bacteria-infested water from ditches.

One survivor later recalled:

"Men dropped by the hundreds, their bodies bloating in the heat. The stench of death followed us every step of the way."

By the time the march ended, between 10,000 to 15,000 POWs had died.

The prisoners who reached Camp O'Donnell expected some relief. Instead, they found a living hell. The camp was overcrowded, with barely enough room to lie down. Disease spread rapidly, with malaria, dysentery, and cholera killing thousands. Food rations were so small that men starved to death in their sleep. Prisoners were beaten for the smallest infractions—sometimes just for looking at a guard the wrong way.

One American soldier later said:

"We envied the dead."

For the next three years, thousands of POWs would endure slave labor, starvation, and torture.

And for many, the nightmare was just beginning.

The Burma Railway: The "Death Railway" of the Pacific

Thousands of Allied POWs were shipped from Southeast Asia to Burma (modern-day Myanmar) and Thailand to work on a massive railway project.

The goal?

To build a 250-mile railway through the jungle, connecting Thailand to Burma. The Japanese needed this railway to transport troops and supplies for their war in India.

The problem?

The railway route cut through dense jungle, mountains, and rivers. No modern equipment was available—everything had to be built by hand.

The solution?

Slave labor. The Japanese forced more than 60,000 Allied POWs and 200,000 Asian laborers to build the railway. And they did so under some of the most horrific conditions imaginable.

Tropical diseases like malaria and dysentery ravaged the prisoners, weakening their bodies as they struggled to survive on a meager handful of rice per day. Malnutrition turned once-strong soldiers into walking skeletons, their bodies wasting away under the relentless conditions. Forced to work 12 to 18 hours a day, often barefoot in the sweltering jungle heat, they endured extreme physical exhaustion. Brutal beatings were a constant threat, with guards mercilessly whipping them with bamboo sticks or striking them with rifle butts for even the smallest mistakes.

One POW later recalled:

"If you collapsed from exhaustion, the guards beat you until you got up. If you couldn't get up, they killed you."

By 1943, the Japanese ordered faster construction—prisoners were told to work at double speed. This period, known as "Speedo" (Speed Month), was the deadliest phase of railway construction.

Thousands of men died of exhaustion and disease. Bodies were buried where they fell, often under the very tracks they built.

Malaysian Tamils during the construction of Death railway between June 1942 to October 1943.

◻ **DID YOU KNOW**

- *This is a shocking figure....in some areas, there was one dead man for every three feet of railway built!*

The Infamous Bridge on the River Kwai

One of the most famous sections of the railway was the Bridge on the River Kwai, a crucial link built by British, Australian, Dutch, and American POWs.

The Japanese forced prisoners to build it under extreme conditions, using crude tools and bare hands. Many men collapsed from overwork, starvation, and disease.

The bridge was eventually bombed by the Allies in 1945, but by then, thousands of men had died building it. The bridge later became the subject of a famous movie, but for those who lived through it, there was nothing cinematic about their suffering.

One British POW, reflecting on his survival, later said:

"We lived through hell, but we never lost our humanity. That was our victory."

◻ DID YOU KNOW

- *Of the 60,000 Allied POWs who worked on the railway, around 16,000 died, a death rate of 27%.*

- *Among the 200,000 Asian laborers, the death toll is estimated at 90,000.*

Wake Island

On October 7, 1943, the Japanese garrison commander, Admiral Shigematsu Sakaibara, gave an order to execute all 98 US civilian construction POWs on Wake Island in reprisal for US air raids. For his role, Sakaibara was executed for war crimes in June 1947.

- *Almost 30,000 American military and civilian personnel were held by the Japanese as POWs during World War II. Almost 11,000 died in captivity, a death rate of 40%!*

- *Over 100,000 British and Commonwealth troops were captured by the Japanese in the Pacific. Around 30,000 died – about 25%, compared with 4% in German camps!*

Hell Ships

POW transport ships, "Hell Ships", were one of the most terrible experiences of POW's captivity. These were Japanese cargo ships that carried Allied POWs to locations throughout the Japanese Empire to be employed as forced labor supporting the war efforts of the Japanese military and civilian corporations. Because the ships were unmarked, many were attacked and sunk by Allied submarines and aircraft with the result that over 21,000 Allied Prisoners of War and Asian forced laborers perished at sea. The Hell Ships remain one of the least known tragedies of the Pacific War.

Conditions aboard the transports were appalling. Hundreds or even thousands of men, wearing little more than rags, were packed, "like sardines in a can" into unlit, unventilated cargo holds. Dysentery spread rapidly as waste flowed throughout the spaces where men ate, lay, and slept.

China and the Three Alls Policy

Japanese soldiers killed millions of non-combatants, including prisoners of war, from surrounding nations. At least 20 million Chinese died during the Second Sino-Japanese War. The Three Alls Policy was responsible for the deaths of more than 2.7 million Chinese civilians - this was a Japanese scorched earth policy, the three "alls" being "kill all, burn all, loot all".

POW Stories of Survival

The Japanese brutalities are now well-known among the horrors of WW2. Less is known about the extraordinary spirit of the prisoners of war - a spirit the cruelty of the Japanese signally failed to conquer.

It is a remarkable story of how they overcame appalling adversity during the war - and how, having survived, they had to do so again in peace because they were so haunted by the horrors they had endured.

Captain Louis Zamperini (U.S. Army Air Forces)

Zamperini, a former Olympic runner, was serving as a bombardier when his plane crashed into the Pacific in 1943. He survived 47 days adrift on a life raft, battling sharks, starvation, and dehydration before being captured by the Japanese. As a POW, he endured relentless beatings and psychological torture, especially from a sadistic guard known as "The Bird."

Captain Louis Zamperini.

Despite the abuse, Zamperini survived and later forgave his captors, a story famously told in Unbroken by Laura Hillenbrand.

Alistair Urquhart (British Army, Gordon Highlanders)

Urquhart was a Scottish soldier captured during the fall of Singapore in 1942. Forced into hard labor on the Burma Railway, he endured starvation, disease, and abuse. He then survived the sinking of a Japanese "Hell Ship" which was torpedoed by an American submarine. Later rescued and reimprisoned, he survived years of maltreatment in Japanese camps until liberation in 1945.

In his book published in 2010, he expresses anger at the lack of recognition in Japan of its role in war crimes compared to the atonement in Germany.

Ernest Gordon (British Army, Argyll and Sutherland Highlanders)

Gordon was captured in 1942 and forced to work on the Thai-Burma Railway, also known as the "Death Railway." Severely malnourished and suffering from multiple diseases, he was left to die in a "death hut." However, fellow prisoners nursed him back to life, and he later helped build a hidden "jungle university" where prisoners taught and educated each other, preserving their dignity despite the horrific conditions.

He survived the war and later wrote Through the Valley of the Kwai, inspiring the film The Bridge on the River Kwai.

Dr. Rowley Richards – The Australian Surgeon of Changi

Dr. Rowley Richards, a young Australian army doctor, became a POW after the fall of Singapore in 1942. He was sent to Changi Prison and later worked on the Thai-Burma Railway under brutal conditions. With almost no medical supplies, he performed surgeries and treated illnesses using whatever he could find, even creating makeshift saline drips from coconut water. His hidden diary, buried in tin cans, later provided a firsthand account of life under Japanese captivity.

Captain Donald Caskie (British Chaplain)

Caskie was a Scottish minister serving as a chaplain for British troops in Southeast Asia. He was captured in Java, where he used his position to secretly aid fellow POWs, smuggling in food and medicine and conducting clandestine religious services. He risked severe punishment to preserve hope among prisoners. Known as the "Tartan Pimpernel," his actions saved lives and spirits.

The Cabanatuan Raid – The Great POW Rescue

By 1945, hundreds of American POWs were still held in the Cabanatuan Camp in the Philippines. Many were survivors of the Bataan Death March. In one of the most daring rescue missions of the war, 121 U.S. Army Rangers and Filipino guerrillas launched a surprise attack, freeing over 500 POWs in just a few hours. The mission was a major morale boost for Allied forces and remains one of the most successful rescue operations in military history.

The Davao Escape – One of the Most Daring POW Breakouts

In April 1943, 10 American POWs and 2 Filipino convicts staged a dramatic escape from the Davao Penal Colony in the Philippines. Led by Lt. William Dyess, they crossed mountains and swamps, evading Japanese patrols with the help of Filipino guerrillas. Their escape was one of the first to reveal the true horrors of Japanese prison camps to the world, helping to expose the Bataan Death March and the mistreatment of Allied prisoners.

War Trials: Holding Japan's leaders accountable.

For the first time in modern history, world leaders were being held accountable for war crimes - both in Nuremberg, Germany, and Tokyo, Japan.

But while both trials aimed for justice, they revealed deep contrasts in how the world viewed war, guilt, and punishment.

The Birth of International War Crimes Trials

Before World War II, there was no clear system for prosecuting war crimes. Leaders who committed mass atrocities often went unpunished.

But after the unimaginable destruction of WWII, the world demanded justice.

Two major trials were held:

- **The Nuremberg Trials (Germany)** – Focused on the Nazi leadership, held from 1945 to 1946.

- **The Tokyo Trials (Japan)** – Focused on Japanese military and political leaders, held from 1946 to 1948.

Both trials were unprecedented.

For the first time in history, high-ranking officials were not just being blamed for war—they were being put on trial for their crimes against humanity.

The Nuremberg Trials: Justice for the Holocaust and War Crimes

The Defendants: The Nazi Leadership on Trial

After Hitler's suicide in April 1945, many of his top lieutenants were captured and placed on trial.

Key figures included:

- Hermann Göring – Hitler's second-in-command and head of the Luftwaffe.
- Rudolf Hess – Hitler's deputy.
- Joachim von Ribbentrop – Foreign Minister responsible for many aggressive policies.
- Wilhelm Keitel – Supreme Commander of the German military.

These men were charged with:

- Crimes against peace (starting an aggressive war).
- War crimes (murder and mistreatment of POWs).
- Crimes against humanity (genocide, including the Holocaust).

The Trial and Verdicts

The trials took place in Nuremberg, Germany, in a courtroom that became the world's stage for justice. The prosecution presented thousands of documents, eyewitness testimonies, and film footage. Survivors of concentration camps described the horrors of Auschwitz, Treblinka, and Dachau, and the world learned, for the first time, the full extent of the Holocaust.

- *The Sentences*

- 12 Nazi leaders were sentenced to death.

- 3 received life imprisonment.

- 4 were given long prison sentences.

- 3 were acquitted (though they remained deeply controversial).

In October 1946, many of the convicted were hanged, including Göring—though he took cyanide poison before his execution.

The Tokyo Trials: Holding Japan's Leaders Accountable

The Defendants: The Faces of Japan's War Machine

The Tokyo Trials, officially called the International Military Tribunal for the Far East (IMTFE), mirrored Nuremberg but focused on Japanese wartime leaders.

- 25 Japanese officials were charged, including:

- General Hideki Tojo – Prime Minister of Japan during WWII.

- Kōichi Kido – Emperor Hirohito's closest advisor.

- Kenji Doihara – Intelligence officer involved in the invasion of China.

Unlike Germany, Japan's leader, Emperor Hirohito, was not put on trial - a decision that remains controversial.

The Charges and the Trial

- The charges against Japan's leaders included:

- Crimes against peace (starting aggressive wars in China, Southeast Asia, and the Pacific).

- War crimes (the Bataan Death March, mass executions, mistreatment of POWs).

- Crimes against humanity (the massacre of civilians, use of biological warfare).

The Tokyo Trials focused on Japan's war against China, the brutal treatment of prisoners, and massacres like the Rape of Nanking.

The Verdicts and Executions

The sentences for Japan's war criminals were severe:

- 7 leaders were sentenced to death, including Tojo.

- 16 received life imprisonment.

- 12 were given shorter sentences.

On December 23, 1948, Hideki Tojo was hanged, along with six others.

Before his execution, Tojo apologized for his role in the war:

> *"I take full responsibility for my actions. May my death bring peace to Japan."*

The Legacy of the Trials: A New Standard for War Crimes

The Nuremberg and Tokyo Trials set the stage for future war crimes prosecutions.

The Geneva Conventions

After WWII, the world created new international laws to protect civilians and prisoners of war. The Geneva Conventions (1949) established clear rules against torture, genocide, and war crimes.

Future War Crimes Trials

The International Criminal Court (ICC) was established to prosecute war crimes in modern conflicts. Trials for war crimes in Bosnia, Rwanda, and Cambodia were directly influenced by the lessons of Nuremberg and Tokyo.

The Message to Future Leaders

Both trials sent a clear warning:

> *"If you commit war crimes, the world will hold you accountable."*

The Human Cost: The Staggering Death Toll of the Pacific War

The Pacific War (1941-1945) was one of the deadliest conflicts in human history, claiming the lives of over 30 million people, including soldiers and civilians, and spreading across China, the Philippines, Japan, Burma, Indonesia, the Pacific Islands, and beyond.

Entire cities were wiped off the map, leaving survivors with nothing but ashes.

Unlike the war in Europe, the Pacific War was often more brutal, with entire populations caught in the crossfire of military campaigns.

The Death Toll by Nation and Region

China: The Forgotten Victims (1937-1945)

The war in the Pacific began long before Pearl Harbor, when Japan invaded China in 1937.

- Over 14 million Chinese people died.

- The Japanese military committed countless atrocities, including:

  - The Rape of Nanking (1937) – over 300,000 civilians were slaughtered.

  - The bombing of Shanghai and Chongqing – thousands of innocent people were killed in aerial raids.

  - Biological warfare – the infamous Unit 731 conducted experiments on prisoners, releasing plagues in villages.

For eight years, China suffered under brutal occupation, with civilians bearing the worst of the war.

The Philippines: A Nation in Flames (1941-1945)

The Battle of the Philippines saw:

- Over 1 million Filipino civilians killed.

- The Bataan Death March, where tens of thousands of American and Filipino POWs died of exhaustion and abuse.

- Entire villages were burned to the ground as Japanese forces conducted massacres.

One survivor later said:

"We were forced to watch as our neighbors were executed. My mother told me to close my eyes, but I could not. The screams haunt me to this day."

The United States and Allied Forces: The Sacrifice of Soldiers

- The U.S. lost over 100,000 troops in the Pacific.

- Battles such as Guadalcanal, Iwo Jima, and Okinawa saw some of the fiercest fighting of the war.

- Many U.S. troops died in POW camps, tortured, starved, or worked to death.

One American soldier, a survivor of the Battle of Guadalcanal, recalled:

> "We lived in a jungle of death. The enemy wasn't just the Japanese—it was the disease, the hunger, the exhaustion. The ground itself was our graveyard."

Japan: A Nation Devastated

The war brought unimaginable suffering to Japan itself.

- Over 2.5 million Japanese soldiers and civilians died.
- Cities like Tokyo, Osaka, and Hiroshima were reduced to ruins.
- The firebombing of Tokyo killed over 100,000 people in a single night.
- The atomic bombings of Hiroshima and Nagasaki killed over 200,000 civilians.

For many Japanese, the war ended not with victory or honor, but with the loss of everything they had ever known.

A survivor from Hiroshima, Setsuko Nakamura, later said:

> "In an instant, my entire world vanished. I had a home. I had a family. And then I had nothing."

The Civilian Experience: Starvation, Bombings, and Survival

The Suffering of Islanders

The Pacific Islands, once a paradise, became battlegrounds of death. Guam, Saipan, and the Solomon Islands were caught between the U.S. and Japan. Entire native populations were displaced, starved, or massacred.

A villager from Saipan remembered:

"We had nowhere to go. The Americans shelled us from the sea, the Japanese forced us to stay. We dug into the earth, hoping to survive another day."

Firebombings and the Destruction of Cities

The firebombing of Tokyo (March 9-10, 1945) was the deadliest air raid in history, killing over 100,000 civilians in one night. Cities across Japan burned, with little left but ashes and corpses.

A survivor described the aftermath:

"The rivers were filled with burned bodies. We had nowhere to run. The air itself was fire."

The Psychological Toll: The Never-Ending War

Even after the war ended, the scars remained. Millions suffered PTSD, unable to escape the memories of war. Survivors of bombings, massacres, and starvation lived with trauma for decades. Many soldiers, both Japanese and American, could never fully return to normal life.

One U.S. Marine, decades later, wrote:

"I never stopped hearing the screams. The war never really ended for me."

CHAPTER 20: THE POST-WAR PACIFIC

The Occupation of Japan: MacArthur's reforms and rebuilding Japan (1945 – 1952)

By Japan's surrender on August 15, 1945, the country was in total collapse. Cities lay in ruins, the economy had crumbled, and the people faced starvation and an uncertain future.

Cities in Ruins

The firebombing of Tokyo in March 1945 killed over 100,000 and left a million homeless. Hiroshima and Nagasaki were obliterated by atomic bombs, with tens of thousands perishing from radiation. Industrial centers, factories, and transportation networks were destroyed, leaving Japan without the means to recover on its own.

Starvation and Economic Collapse

With farms bombed and food supplies crippled, rationing had already left millions malnourished. After the surrender, food shipments stopped entirely, pushing the nation to the brink of famine. Inflation soared, making even basic necessities unaffordable.

The Psychological Toll of Defeat

For years, the Japanese had been taught that dying for the Emperor was the highest honor. Now, their country had surrendered. Soldiers returned to find their homes gone and families missing or dead. Many felt lost and humiliated, unsure of their place in this new reality.

The Fate of the Emperor

Emperor Hirohito, once worshipped as a god, now faced an uncertain future. Some in the U.S. wanted him tried as a war criminal, but General Douglas MacArthur made the controversial decision to let him remain as Emperor - on the condition that he renounce his divine status. In his first public speech after the war, Hirohito declared:

> *"The Emperor is not divine. He is but a human ruler of the Japanese people."*

For many Japanese, this revelation was more shocking than the war itself. But Japan had to move forward - and MacArthur had a plan.

General Douglas MacArthur: The Man Who Rebuilt Japan

General Douglas MacArthur was no ordinary commander. Having led U.S. forces in the Pacific and fulfilled his famous promise to return to the Philippines, he was now named Supreme Commander of the Allied Powers (SCAP), granting him absolute authority over Japan. His mission was clear: rebuild Japan, reform its government, and ensure it would never wage war again. But instead of punishing the defeated nation, MacArthur took a different approach—one focused on reconstruction, democracy, and economic revival.

Political Reform: A New Democratic Government

One of the most significant changes was Japan's transformation from a militaristic empire to a democracy. In 1947, a new constitution - known as the "MacArthur Constitution" - was introduced. It established a parliamentary government modeled after Britain's system and granted universal suffrage, allowing Japanese women to vote for the first time. The constitution also guaranteed freedoms of speech, religion, and assembly while abolishing the military and forbidding Japan from waging war, except in self-defense. These reforms permanently reshaped Japan's political landscape.

Economic Reform: Rebuilding Japan's Industry

With its economy in ruins, Japan needed rapid industrialization. MacArthur's administration implemented land reforms that redistributed farmland, empowering small farmers over landlords. Labor unions were encouraged, improving wages and working conditions. The U.S. also provided billions in aid to rebuild factories and infrastructure, laying the foundation for Japan's future economic boom.

War Crimes Trials: Justice for the Pacific War

While Emperor Hirohito was spared, Japan's military leaders were held accountable. The Tokyo Trials (1946–1948) prosecuted those responsible for war crimes, resulting in seven executions, including former Prime Minister Hideki Tojo. Others received life sentences for atrocities such as massacres, forced labor, and mistreatment of POWs. While many saw the trials as justice, some criticized them for not punishing all war criminals equally.

Social Reform: Changing Japanese Culture

To prevent the resurgence of militarism, MacArthur's administration enacted sweeping cultural reforms. Education was modernized to emphasize peace, democracy, and science instead of military values. Censorship was lifted, allowing for open discussion in the media. Women gained new rights, including the ability to vote, work, and receive an education. These reforms transformed Japan into a more progressive and open society, setting the stage for its postwar recovery and modernization.

▫ **DID YOU KNOW**

- *The new Japanese Constitution (1947) renounced war and forbade Japan from having a military. However, during the Cold War, the U.S. encouraged Japan to create the Japan Self-Defense Forces (JSDF).*

Japan's Economic Miracle: The Rise of a Superpower

By the 1950s and 1960s, Japan underwent one of the most remarkable economic recoveries in history. The country rapidly industrialized, becoming a global leader in electronics, automobiles, and advanced technology. Companies like Sony, Toyota, and Honda emerged as dominant brands worldwide. By the 1980s, Japan had grown into the world's second-largest economy, a transformation rooted in the reforms implemented during the U.S. occupation.

The End of the Occupation: Japan Regains Independence

On April 28, 1952, the Treaty of San Francisco officially ended the U.S. occupation, restoring Japan's sovereignty. However, Japan remained closely allied with the United States, which maintained military bases in the country to ensure its security during the Cold War. This alliance continues today, a lasting outcome of MacArthur's leadership and post-war reforms.

The Legacy of the Occupation

Japan's post-war transformation had long-term global significance. The country never returned to militarism, instead emerging as one of the world's strongest democracies. Its economic policies fueled rapid growth, turning Japan into a global leader in technology, business, and innovation. The success of the U.S. occupation also became a model for rebuilding war-torn nations, influencing American policies in Germany, South Korea, and Iraq.

▫ *DID YOU KNOW*

- *Baseball helped rebuild Japan. American teams, including Babe Ruth and later MLB stars, played exhibition games, helping to improve U.S.-Japan relations.*

- *The main occupation ended in 1952, but the U.S. kept control of Okinawa until 1972. Even today, the U.S. maintains a large military presence in Japan, especially in Okinawa.*

The Fall of European Empires in Asia: Decolonization and Independence

Before World War II, much of Asia remained under European colonial rule. Britain controlled India, Burma, Malaya, and Singapore, while the Dutch ruled Indonesia, the French governed Indochina (Vietnam, Laos, and Cambodia), and the Americans held the Philippines. For centuries, these colonies were exploited for resources and labor, but Japan's invasion in 1941–1942 changed everything.

The Japanese Occupation: Shattering the Myth of European Supremacy

Japan's rapid conquests in Asia exposed the vulnerability of European colonial powers. The British lost Malaya and Singapore in just 70 days, the Dutch surrendered Indonesia with little resistance, and the French were driven out of Indochina. For many Asians, this proved that European rule was not invincible. Despite Japan's own harsh occupation, its victories planted the seeds of revolution, fueling nationalist movements across the region.

The Rise of Nationalism During the War

As Japanese forces occupied Asia, nationalist movements gained momentum. Japan supported leaders like Sukarno in Indonesia and Aung San in Burma to undermine European control. Many Asians saw firsthand that they could resist colonial rule, and groups like the Indian National Army (INA) emerged to challenge European dominance. When the war ended, former colonial rulers tried to reclaim their territories, but nationalist sentiment had become too strong.

Independence Movements Across Asia

India (1947): The End of British Rule

India, Britain's most prized colony, became impossible to hold after the war. Mahatma Gandhi's nonviolent resistance movement and the Indian National Army's military campaign had shaken British authority. With Britain's economy weakened, maintaining control was no longer feasible. On August 15, 1947, India gained independence, but the moment was overshadowed by the partition into India and Pakistan, triggering mass migration and violence that claimed over a million lives.

Indonesia (1945–1949): Struggle Against the Dutch

Indonesia declared independence on August 17, 1945, under nationalist leaders Sukarno and Mohammad Hatta. However, the Dutch attempted to reclaim their colony, leading to a brutal four-year war. Under international pressure, the Netherlands finally recognized Indonesia's independence in 1949. This victory reinforced the determination of other Asian nations to break free from colonial rule.

Vietnam (1945–1954): War Against French Rule

On September 2, 1945, Ho Chi Minh proclaimed Vietnam's independence from France. The French, unwilling to let go of Indochina, launched a war to reclaim it. The First Indochina War lasted until 1954, culminating in the French defeat at Dien Bien Phu. Vietnam was then divided into North and South, setting the stage for the Vietnam War. The struggle in Vietnam became one of the bloodiest independence movements of the 20th century.

Burma (1948): Aung San's Vision of Freedom

In Burma, Aung San, leader of the Burmese National Army, initially allied with Japan against the British but later switched sides. After the war, Burma negotiated its independence, which was granted in 1948. Tragically, Aung San was assassinated before he could witness the nation's freedom, and Burma soon fell into decades of internal conflict.

Malaya and Singapore (1957–1965): The Path to Independence

Britain's grip on Malaya, rich in rubber and tin, faced resistance from a communist-led insurgency known as the Malayan Emergency. After years of conflict, Malaya gained independence in 1957, followed by Singapore in 1965. Singapore's transformation into one of the world's most prosperous nations demonstrated that post-colonial states could thrive.

The End of European Rule in Asia

The war shattered the illusion of colonial invincibility, empowered nationalist movements, and made it clear that Asian nations would no longer accept foreign domination. By the mid-20th century, much of the continent had won independence, marking the end of centuries of European rule, and reshaping Asia.

The Global Impact of Decolonization in Asia

The end of European colonial rule in Asia reshaped global power dynamics. By the 1960s, nearly all Asian nations had gained independence, marking the collapse of British, French, and Dutch dominance in the region, and set the stage for new political and economic transformations.

Asia as a Cold War Battleground

With independence came new challenges, as many Asian nations found themselves caught in the Cold War struggle between the United States and the Soviet Union. Vietnam and Korea became major battlegrounds in the ideological conflict between communism and capitalism, while countries like Indonesia faced internal struggles influenced by the global superpowers. The fight for independence was often followed by another struggle - choosing a path in a divided world.

Economic Transformation and Growth

While some nations struggled with post-colonial instability, others embraced rapid industrialization and economic reform. Japan, South Korea, and Singapore emerged as global economic powerhouses, proving that newly independent nations could thrive. Others, like Vietnam, endured years of conflict and reconstruction before achieving stability.

The colonial empires had vanished, and in their place, a new world order had begun - one shaped by Cold War tensions, economic growth, and the determination of independent nations to define their own futures.

The old empires were gone.

A new world order had begun.

LESSONS FROM THE PACIFIC WAR

The Pacific War was one of the deadliest conflicts in history, but its impact did not end in 1945. It reshaped the world politically, economically, and culturally, leaving behind lessons that remain relevant today. The war was more than a battle between nations—it was a struggle over power, ideology, and the future of global stability.

The War's Role in Shaping the Modern World

By the war's end, two nations had been profoundly transformed.

The United States: The Rise of a Superpower

Before World War II, the U.S. was a major economic force but not yet the dominant global leader it would become. Victory in the Pacific and Europe secured its position as the world's leading military power. The U.S. established military bases across the Pacific, ushering in an era of global influence. The atomic bombings of Hiroshima and Nagasaki signaled the start of the nuclear age, with America at the forefront.

The war also brought social change within the U.S. Women and minorities played vital roles in the workforce and military, paving the way for civil rights movements. The post-war economic boom fueled prosperity and shaped the "American Dream." From this point forward, the United States was not just a nation—it was the leader of the free world.

Japan: From Militarism to Peace

Few nations have undergone a greater transformation than Japan after World War II. In 1945, its cities lay in ruins, its economy had collapsed, and millions were left homeless. However, under U.S. occupation and General Douglas MacArthur's leadership, Japan underwent one of the most remarkable national rebuildings in history.

A new democratic government replaced the militaristic regime, and the Emperor renounced his divine status, shifting power to elected officials. Japan's military was abolished, and a new pacifist constitution ensured the country would never wage war again. With U.S. support, Japan rebuilt its economy and, by the 1960s, had become an industrial powerhouse. Most remarkably, Japan transformed from a military empire into one of the most peaceful nations on Earth.

Lessons from the Conflict

The Pacific War revealed both the darkest and most resilient aspects of humanity. It showed how unchecked ambition and nationalism could lead to devastation but also how unity and determination could rebuild shattered nations.

The Dangers of Militarism and Nationalism

Japan's leaders pursued expansion at any cost, believing their nation was destined to rule Asia. They silenced opposition, ignored diplomacy, and justified war as a path to glory. By the time Japan surrendered, over 30 million people had died, and the country was nearly destroyed. The lesson is clear: unchecked militarism leads to destruction, and war should never be seen as a solution.

The Power of Rebuilding and Reconciliation

Despite the war's brutality, former enemies became allies. The United States and Japan, once sworn foes, developed one of the closest economic and political partnerships in modern history. Germany followed a similar path, proving that even nations devastated by war could rebuild and forge peaceful futures. This transformation reminds us that no conflict is truly permanent and that even the deepest wounds can be healed.

The Cost of War and the Value of Peace

The Pacific War demonstrated the horrors of modern warfare. The firebombing of Tokyo killed more civilians than the atomic bombings, and millions suffered through starvation, massacres, and war crimes. The devastation made it clear that war is not just about soldiers and battles—it destroys families, communities, and futures. Diplomacy and conflict resolution must always be prioritized because history has shown that while war is easy to start, its consequences can last for generations.

The Importance of Remembering History

As time passes, memories fade, and the voices of those who lived through the war grow fewer. But we must never forget.

Honoring Sacrifices

Soldiers who fought in battles like Iwo Jima, Guadalcanal, and Okinawa risked their lives with no certainty of return. Civilians endured bombings, starvation, and occupation. Prisoners of war survived unimaginable hardships in places like Bataan and Changi prison camps. Their sacrifices shaped the world we live in today, and we owe it to them to remember and learn from their experiences.

History as a Guide for the Future

The past is not just a record - it is a warning. If we forget the dangers of unchecked power, we risk repeating the same mistakes. If we ignore the lessons of war, new conflicts may arise. And if we fail to value peace, we may lose it before realizing its worth.

The Pacific War was a lesson written in blood - one that must never be forgotten.

Thank you for reading!

If you enjoyed this book, I would be grateful if you could share your thoughts in a review on Amazon.

If you want to read more, then you can find all my books at james-burrows.com and follow me on Instagram at @burrowsauthor.

Thank you!

ABOUT THE AUTHOR

I am a passionate military and history writer whose love for the past was kindled by family stories. One grandfather endured four years as a prisoner of war in Poland during World War 2, while my great-grandfather fought at the Somme in World War 1 — a legacy that ignited a lifelong fascination with courage, conflict, and the human spirit in wartime.

In 2024, after receiving a diagnosis of stage 4 cancer, I turned to writing with newfound purpose. The act of storytelling has become a welcome distraction for me! As of July 2025, I've completed 34 cycles of fortnightly chemotherapy, a treatment that continues — but so does my writing, undeterred and determined.

Whether I'm exploring the battles of World War II, the legends of Greek mythology, the intrigue of Roman emperors, or the ambition of Alexander the Great, I write to inspire curiosity in readers, both young and old, and make history come alive with meaning.

I live in the Cotswolds with my wife, my two children, and two lovely black Labradors. When not writing or reading, you'll likely find me wandering the hills dreaming up my next journey into the past.

See more at: ***james-burrows.com and @burrowsauthor***.

If you enjoyed this book, I'd appreciate a review – please scan the QR Code below:

If you'd like to read more, you can find all my books at:

www.ingramcontent.com/pod-product-compliance
Lightning Source LLC
Chambersburg PA
CBHW071157070526
44584CB00019B/2820